DEBBY BOONE

So Far

DEBBY BOONE

So Far

by
Debby Boone
with
Dennis Baker

THOMAS NELSON PUBLISHERS
Nashville

Published in Nashville, Tennessee, by Thomas Nelson, Inc., Publishers and
distributed in Canada by Lawson Falle, Ltd., Cambridge, Ontario.

Printed in the United States of America.

The Scripture quotations in this publication are from the Revised Standard
Version of the Bible, copyrighted 1946, 1952, © 1971, 1973 by the Division of
Christian Education of the National Council of the Churches of Christ in the
U.S.A., and used by permission.

The description of the angel Gabriel on page 162 is from *The Interpreter's
Dictionary of The Bible*, 5 vols. (Nashville, Tenn.: Abingdon, 1976).

The description of Deborah on page 162ff was adapted from Hebert Lockyer's
The Women of the Bible (Grand Rapids, Mich.: Zondervan, 1967) p. 40ff.

ISBN 0-8407-4092-1

2145538

Contents

DEBBY
BOONE

So Far

Introduction

"What do you have to write a book about?" A few of my closer friends have been bold enough to ask me that out loud. Many more have surely wondered it to themselves. Some of the more cynical among them have probably concluded, "Well, Debby You-Light-Up-My-Life Boone has found one more way to cash in on the success of her record."

Frankly, when the idea of doing a book was first presented to me, I was skeptical—mostly because I, too, wondered what I would have to say. I thought about the celebrity books that are so popular, full of torrid love affairs and incriminating revelations about family members or fellow entertainers. I didn't have any of those things to offer, unless my book were to be largely fictitious. So, I had to ask myself, "What, if anything, do I have to offer?"

My first response was, "Nothing," so my answer to the first request that I write a book was "no." I must confess, however, that my decision was heavily influenced by the fact that writing never has come easily to me. In school, I found it painstakingly tedious work and, in fact, handed in more of my three sisters' work than my own.

Well, here you are reading an introduction to my book; so unless the remaining one hundred and some odd pages are blank, I obviously must have found something to write about. What changed my mind? A few things really. Primarily it was the ever-increasing amount of mail I was receiving. Unlike most fan mail, which consists of requests for autographed pictures, birthdates, favorite colors, etc., the majority of my mail was, and continues to be, very personal. People of every age share with me intimate details of their lives, both good and bad, because they either relate to me on some level or they want my advice concerning their problems. More often than not, I learn later that my answers to those letters have helped a great deal. That is very rewarding to me.

So I figured that even though I wouldn't be writing a Nobel Prize winner, if writing about my experiences could help somebody, or even just be good company to someone going through some of the same things, it would be a worthwhile project.

I didn't write this book for a large audience, but for just one person—you, I hope. What follows is not an autobiography, but it is a chance for me to sit with you and share the stories of some of the more important things that have happened in my life. I trust you'll find it interesting. But more than that, I pray you'll be encouraged as you face your own points of conflict and struggle, because, as you'll see, there is a way through and out of them.

Daddy and Me

"What did you do with those cigarette butts? Did you smoke them?"

It was my father, who had awakened me out of a sound sleep. I rolled over and sat up in bed. My sister Lindy was watching from beneath the covers across the room. We were in a hotel in Tokyo. I was fifteen. Daddy stood at the foot of my bed, fists placed demandingly on his hips as he glared at me.

"Why do you *always* pick on me?" I screamed back. "Why don't you ever yell at the others when you think one of us has done something?"

"Think about it, Debby. How many times have I found cigarettes in your room or caught you smoking? Who else would it be?" He turned abruptly and stormed out of the room, then shouted from the hall, "I'll deal with you later!" The door slammed shut behind him.

I ran into the adjoining room and found Cherry sitting up in her bed, awakened by all the noise.

"*I hate him,*" I seethed. "He's so unfair. It's always my fault whenever anything goes wrong. Why always me? Why never any of you?"

"Was it you?" Cherry asked.

"Yes, it was me, but he didn't even give me a chance! What if it hadn't been me and he had barged in accusing me like that?"

I flung myself down on the edge of the bed, choking back tears.

"He wouldn't have believed me, even if I hadn't smoked those stupid cigarettes. He doesn't even try to understand me. He doesn't care what I want. I can't wait until I can get away from him!"

Cherry's eyes filled with tears as I trembled in rage. She could tell that these were not just words. My hate was very real. I looked up at her and saw on her face a mixture of sadness and pain.

"Debby, how can you talk like that?" Now she began to cry in earnest. She took my hand and pulled me into the bathroom, so we could let Laury, my younger sister, sleep. "Sit down there on the floor, and be quiet and listen to me." Her voice was firm. Obediently I sat and listened.

"Now look, Debby. I know what it's like. And I admit that Daddy doesn't always handle situations the best way possible. But I swear to you, his motives are right."

"He's smothering me!"

"He *loves* you. He's concerned and he's trying to raise us the best way possible. He wants *so much* to protect you from danger. All kinds—physical, emotional, *and* spiritual. He's just trying to save you from making mistakes that could really hurt you. Can't you see that? If he didn't care. . . ."

"Love? Restrictions, accusations, rules, spankings—that's all I see! I don't see any love. I hate being in trouble all the time. I hate not being allowed to do anything fun. I hate being accused of every darn thing that happens. I hate. . . ."

"Just calm down, Debby. Try to think. Does he go to all that trouble and get that angry with you because he doesn't care about you?"

"I don't know, Cherry. But I do know it doesn't feel like love."

"Maybe not. But tell the truth, Deb. Does he really get angry very often? I mean really explode?"

"No, but when he does, he gets crazy. I hate it."

"You know something? Sometimes I've watched you drive

him to it. He'll be correcting you about something, and you'll give him that look with your eyes. Then, when you get Daddy to explode, you can point your finger at him and get everybody's attention off what you did in the first place."

"But he doesn't understand me. His opinions don't carry any weight with me anymore. They don't make any sense. I feel like I have to raise myself, so who needs. . . ."

"*You* do. We're a family, and we all need each other. Let me tell you something Mom told me a couple of weeks ago. She and Daddy were kneeling by their bed praying. Daddy was so upset by all the trouble between you and him that he was weeping and crying out to God to show him how to communicate with you."

"Really?"

I thought about how things had been going, especially during the last year. I had begun to decide I was old enough to handle life on my own. I certainly didn't want any part of my parents' embarrassing rules. I had withdrawn into a world of my own where I thought I could find out who I really was. I refused affection. I didn't want anyone to touch me. There were nights when I retreated to my room and cried for hours, letting feelings of resentment and hatred build up inside me.

Naturally, my parents' first reaction was to worry, and then it seemed as if their feelings for me began to cool.

I thought sometimes about my father's past problems. When I was much younger, he had thought his career was sliding downhill. Losing money and believing that renewed success required joining the Hollywood social set, Daddy began spending a lot of time at parties, learning to drink, gamble, and flirt. When he started to ignore his family, quarrels with my mother became more frequent. Then things changed. But why should I have to abide by his rigid rules, I thought, when he hadn't? He was no better than a hypocrite.

Now I had to think again. It was hard to call him a hypocrite and, at the same time, to think of him praying and crying about me. As I envisioned him on his knees like that, something in me broke.

Cherry and I talked a long time that night. Her sincerity and conviction had touched me. It was nearly dawn when I finally admitted that maybe—just maybe—I didn't hate him.

To Cherry, that was a great victory.

In a way, it isn't hard to understand why my dad thought of me when he and Mom came back from dinner and discovered that all the reporters' cigarette butts had vanished. He and I had been at odds for about three years. I resented his authority in my life. In fact, I resented most people who presumed to tell me what to do or how to do it.

The person who presumed the most in that way was my dad. My sisters and I had to account for every minute we spent away from home. None of us was allowed to date until we were sixteen, and then our boyfriends almost had to fill out a minute-by-minute itinerary before they could take us out of the house.

Nor were we allowed to wear makeup until we were sixteen. Any movies we wanted to go to had to be approved. Our TV watching was censored. In fact, all our activities were carefully supervised and restricted.

I remember, though, that I really began to resent my parents just after my twelfth birthday. I was about to enter the sixth grade when my parents decided to send me to a different school. Cherry and Laury had already been there a year, and now Lindy and I would join them. I was not pleased. I had started to get interested in boys, and my old school was coeducational. The new one was for girls only. Then there were the usual hassles that come with adapting to a new environment and feeling the loss of something old and familiar.

Once I actually began attending the school, the fire of my resentment grew. I was having a very rough time making decent grades, and I hated the fact that I had to follow in the wake of my two older sisters, who were model students. It seemed like I was always studying for some test or hurrying

to finish some overdue report. I can't even count the times I
came home in tears with a big red "C–" or "D" etched on the
front page of my paper. I felt mistreated for having to go to a
school I didn't like. I also thought it unfair that I was loaded
down with so much work that there was little time for anything else. All of this contributed to the tension between my
parents and me.

Not only had they disrupted my life by sending me to this
new school, their rules made me stand out like a sore thumb.
I was one of a handful of girls in the entire school who wore
skirts below the knees, and I was the only one in my class
who wasn't allowed to go to parties at night.

My father and I clashed constantly. He didn't seem to
understand me. I would get spanked for what he called "glaring" at him. We would be fighting about something, and he
would grab my face and shove it towards a mirror. "Do you
see that look? Do you think that's pretty? *Do you?*" In an
instant, the look would change; my face would soften. "What
look?" I would ask demurely. "I'm sorry if you don't like my
face, but it's the only one I've got."

The flare-ups continued through high school. Even when I
was in the tenth grade, Daddy censored my reading material.
It was just another example of what I considered his embarrassing dominance. When my class was assigned to read
Eldridge Cleaver's book, *Soul On Ice*, Daddy went to school
with me and confronted my teacher.

"Why do you want fifteen- and sixteen-year-old girls to
read material with such graphic descriptions of sex and erotic
fantasy?" Daddy asked him.

The teacher got a real condescending look on his face and
said, "Look, Mr. Boone, don't you know that any kid can go
to a newsstand, pick up this book, and read it? A lot of them
already have. Wouldn't you rather your daughter read and
discuss this book in class with some kind of guidance?"

"No," Daddy said, pointing out that his daughter wouldn't
have the opportunity to read the entire book under any cir-

cumstances. He suggested that the teacher assign excerpts from the book which were important and exclude the parts that were pornographic.

Daddy finally let me read parts of *Soul On Ice,* but only after he'd taped all the objectionable pages together. So there I was, going to school every morning, carrying around my taped-up book and trying to hide it from my friends.

School continued to be a problem, both from the standpoint of my grades and my father's interference with the curriculum. He objected to some of the movies shown as part of a literature course. When the X-rated *A Clockwork Orange* was scheduled, he claimed the school was breaking the law. And then there was the time I got a long lecture when rumors circulated that one teacher, who invited students to his apartment, was smoking pot and passing it around.

I didn't feel like part of any group. With what I considered my father's overprotective attitude and with all his rules interfering with my life, I doubted if I would fit in anywhere.

As my parents continued to structure my life, my resentment grew. I was constantly looking for ways to get around the no-makeup, no-unapproved-movies, no-dating rules. Frustrated because it was difficult to break the rules without getting caught and punished, I began thinking about running away.

The movie *Easy Rider* was released about that time, and the movie's publicity posters gave me the idea of hitching a ride on someone's motorcycle, preferably a "chopper"—I really wanted to ride on one of those bikes with the long, rakish front ends—and go to San Francisco. Descriptions of Haight-Asbury sounded like heaven.

I never left Beverly Hills, but I did begin smoking and drinking secretly. Many of my friends had a lot of freedom. I hid cigarettes everywhere—in the garden and around the house—so that whenever I had the chance I could go for a walk or to a friend's house and smoke. Alcohol was harder to come by, but there were ways to get around that.

My father's attempts to resolve the problem only made it

worse. His increasing concern was met with my increasing indifference. When I would come home from school, he'd try to put his arm around me and ask me how my day was. I would shrink away from his touch and not answer him.

Finally, one night around the dinner table, as I sat in my silent anger, my mother asked me, "Don't you love us?" I pushed my food around with my fork and said nothing. "Can't you even say, 'I love you'?" she asked with alarm.

"Why should I have to say that?"

"But why not, honey?"

"I shouldn't have to say something like that on demand. If I say it, it should come spontaneously. This is phony. I'm not a little windup doll that says what you want to hear when you want to hear it." I felt it was simply a contest of wills, and I was bound and determined my mother would not win.

She took hold of my shoulders and began to cry. "Please say, 'I love you.' *Please.*" I got up from the table quietly and walked into the den. From there, as I sat in the enveloping darkness, I could hear my mother's sobs in the next room.

In later years, my dad and mom wrote about what they went through during that time in a book entitled *The Honeymoon Is Over*. Thinking about me, my dad observed, "My run-ins with Cherry seem minor league compared to the head-on collisions I had with Debby" (p. 58). Mom added that I hated school more than any of my sisters had. Then they both went on to describe some of the incidents that illustrated the intensity of our conflict.

There was another side of me that, standing next to my strong inclination to rebellion, didn't make sense to them. My dad put it this way, "The amazing thing was that Debby would come home from school and ask Shirley and me to pray for one or another of her friends!" (p. 60). It was true. Some of my friends—one in particular—were beginning to experiment with marijuana. That really upset me, and I asked my folks to pray with me for her. And it worked. My friend and I were able to talk and pray together after that, and she gave it up.

My faith was real to me. From earliest childhood, I had been taught about Jesus and His love for me. I had asked Him to come into my heart and live there as my Savior. As I grew up, I learned to rely on God as the One who truly loved me and cared for me. But, somehow, I managed to keep matters of faith distinct from questions of obedience and submission to authority.

It was an arrangement that could never last. Faith and rebellion can't live in the same house indefinitely. Either one or the other will finally achieve dominance and drive the other out. But when I was in my teens, I didn't recognize that fact. Instead, I loved Jesus and hated my father, and I saw little or no conflict between those two postures.

Kevin

Tension between my dad and me was pretty steady during much of my childhood. When I moved into adolescence, the conflicts grew more intense. And when it came to boys, Daddy and I really clashed.

Brian was my first boyfriend. Actually, we had known one another since early childhood, because our parents were close friends. That helped keep Daddy off my back a little bit when Brian and I got to feeling romantic about each other, just after I turned fourteen. Brian was sixteen, and we were part of a group that went to a Jesus festival. It was there that our old childhood boy-girl hostility gave way to my first romance.

Brian was tender and attentive. When I felt ugly and self-conscious because my complexion was in trouble and my long arms were covered with freckles, he regularly insisted I was beautiful. He wrote love songs to me and songs for me to sing. He became my confidant and closest friend. Sometimes we talked about the future and maybe getting married. In fact, it seemed like a sure thing. But after several years of getting to know each other, our relationship gradually dwindled and disappeared. Seeing our romance end was difficult for both of us, but I always remember our friendship very fondly.

Regardless of the outcome, though, it was Brian who first endured with me my parents' iron grip of supervision over my social life. Like most teenagers, we talked endlessly on the phone. Unlike most teenagers, that was where our relationship was the most romantically expressive. Whenever we were actually in each other's company, my father or mother was sure to be somewhere very near at hand.

Only after two years of being boyfriend and girlfriend were we allowed to leave the premises on an honest-to-goodness date. That, of course, was on my sixteenth birthday. We looked forward to it as if we were prisoners looking ahead to the day of release.

Brian arrived that evening dressed very nicely. I wore a pretty new outfit I had received from my parents for my birthday. I ran to get the door when the bell rang, but Daddy beat me to it. There he was, shaking Brian's hand.

"Well, don't the two of you look great," Daddy said with a smile as I walked up. "Wait here a minute while I get the camera. Gotta have a picture of you looking this good."

Daddy always had to get in his little jabs. He didn't like the way I normally dressed, in faded jeans and sloppy shirts.

I didn't have time to reply, because Mom came swishing into the room. "Hi, Brian! This is the big night, huh? You two have a good time."

"Yes, ma'am."

Daddy came back with camera and exhortations to smile. It became a major production. By the time they finally let us out the door, I felt as if I had a smile painted on my face.

The big scene before we left embarrassed me. As far as I was concerned, this date should have taken place two years before. I resented not being allowed to date, and just because I was finally sixteen and walking out the door didn't mean all was forgiven and forgotten.

In the privacy of Brian's car, I let loose. "Could you believe it? I thought they were going to make you sign a sworn statement that you would have me home by eleven!"

"You're not kidding! And the show won't even be over till ten."

Despite all the hassles and the intolerably early curfew, we actually had time for a pleasant and leisurely dinner—and a toast with a bit of forbidden champagne—before time for the show. My home wasn't far, so after the performance we had nearly an hour to linger privately in each other's company before I had to be home.

When Brian delivered me to the door at 10:59 my parents were right there waiting for us. It was almost as if they hadn't moved since saying goodbye to us several hours before. I wasn't really surprised. I had watched it happen with my two older sisters, and I had no reason to expect they would change policy for me—least of all, me.

As time passed after that momentous first date, I learned to expect one of two things whenever I arrived home from a date. If I took the guy inside, we'd soon hear Daddy whistling or humming—his musical signal that it was time to end the evening. If we stayed outside, the porch and yard lights would soon start flashing. Sometimes I was sure we were just plain spied on. One day, I came in after having spent some time walking with Brian in our backyard. We had kissed and embraced a few times as we stood there saying goodbye.

My mom greeted me at the door; her expression intense. "Now, Debby, I just happened to be in the den and I noticed you two hugging and kissing in the yard. Of course, there's nothing too wrong with that, but what if Laury had seen you? I think you ought to consider what sort of example you're setting for your younger sister."

I was furious. As far as I was concerned, it was unfair to drag in Laury and what kind of example I was to her, especially when I was sure the real issue was that my mother didn't trust me.

Most of the time, in fact, she had little to worry about. I grew up among people who believed that sex was reserved for marriage. Most of the guys I went out with respected my position. There was one, however, who nearly got me to change my mind.

I was seventeen and had recently broken up with Brian when I met a very intriguing older man. Kevin was a hairdresser working at the studio where my family was filming a commercial for Japanese television. He was very attractive and started showing interest after I joked and flirted with him for several days. On the last day of shooting, he said he wanted to see me again and asked for my phone number. I was flattered and, as he was fourteen years older, I felt very adult.

"Who was that on the phone? Was it Brian?" Mom's normal curiosity was as strong as ever that day.

"No, it was Kevin. Remember? He's the hairdresser I met last week when we were doing that Japanese commercial."

"Oh? What did he want?"

"Nothing much. He just called to see how I was."

"How did he get your number?"

"I gave it to him on the last day of the commercial. Why?"

"Well, as I remember he's quite a bit older than you. Does he want to take you out?"

"We talked about it a little bit."

"How old is he, anyway?"

"Thirty-one."

"He's nearly twice your age."

"Oh, Mom! Why do you always have to exaggerate?"

"What's going on in here?" I think Daddy had overheard us. Anyway, he chose this moment to join us in the kitchen, and I was outnumbered.

Mom spoke next. "Remember that guy on the set of the Japanese commercial—the hairdresser?" My father nodded as Mom continued. "He wants to take Debby out, and he's thirty-one years old."

"That's too old."

"Hey, wait a second. You hardly even know him."

"Look, Deb, you're too young and inexperienced to handle yourself with a man that old."

"That's unfair! You're not even giving us a chance."

"Deb, I'm really sorry you feel that way about it. But what

can I do? I would be very irresponsible if I let my seventeen-year-old go out with a guy fourteen years older."

I retreated to my bedroom. I didn't want Mom and Dad to see the tears of frustration they'd provoked. I was so angry I wanted to scream. Every time I turned around, it seemed, there they were—saying no. *What do they expect?* I thought. Was I supposed to sit in my room playing with dolls until they found the perfect date for me?

I talked with Kevin on the phone just a few days after that. Afterward, as I was enjoying the good feeling that came with his special attention, I resolved anew to get my dad's permission to go out with him.

"What difference does it make when two people like each other? Age isn't important," I argued.

"Sometimes it's not. I'll grant you that, but it is usually when the age difference is between two older people. There's another problem that worries me. I don't think Kevin's a Christian, is he?"

"No, he told me he was kind of an agnostic."

"Well, you know what the Bible says—'Be not unequally yoked with unbelievers.' "

"I don't want to get under a yoke with him. I just want to go out on a simple date."

"There's nothing simple about going out on a date with a man in his thirties who acknowledges no authority in his life other than his own."

"How's he ever going to have a chance to hear about the gospel if he never spends time with Christian people? His wanting to go out with me may just be the opportunity for me to talk to him about Jesus."

"Kevin has been around a lot longer than you have, Debby. There's no way you're going to have the stronger influence in the relationship."

"Why do you keep harping on our age difference? You admitted it doesn't always make a difference when two people really like each other."

"You better watch that tone of voice." Daddy's patience

was beginning to wane. "Why is this so important to you? You've only talked to the guy on the phone."

"That doesn't mean I don't have real feelings. I just want a chance to spend some time with a mature person. Maybe that will help me sort out my feelings."

But Daddy remained adamant. There was no way he was going to let Kevin take me out alone—or any other way, for that matter. I was banging my head against a brick wall. There was nothing to do but change tactics.

I dropped the subject for several days to allow things to cool down a bit. I also made sure Kevin wouldn't call, except when I knew my parents and sisters wouldn't be within earshot. Then, gradually, around the family I began to talk and act as if my feelings for Kevin had become much less intense. I spread the word that I only wanted to be friends with him, nothing more.

When I sensed that Daddy had let his guard down a bit, I approached him again about letting me see Kevin. I didn't use the word *date*. The whole thing was as casual as I could manage. And it worked! A little bit.

"I don't suppose it would hurt anything for you to see him," Daddy said. I could hardly believe my ears! I was so excited . . . until he went on to elaborate what he meant by my having a chance to see Kevin. "I'll tell you what. If he'd like to come over here for dinner with the family, or if he'd like to go to church with us some Sunday, I think we could arrange for you to have some time together under those circumstances." Daddy looked at me expectantly.

"Oh, thanks," I said weakly. I tried to picture Kevin at one of our family dinners, or, worse yet, at one of our church's demonstrative worship services. I shuddered. Both were impossible. Those were not aspects of my life I wanted to share with Kevin—too embarrassing. Actually, as stubbornly as I asserted that our age difference made no difference, I was nevertheless secretly afraid it would make a difference to Kevin. If he found out how strictly I was regulated, like a child, he might lose interest. Daddy had been entirely sincere and had, in his eyes, made quite a concession. But I was still banging my head against that wall.

I left town on a family vacation without seeing or even talking with Kevin. But as soon as I returned, I wrote to him and told him about my father's offer. I figured that would be the end, but Kevin called and said that would be fine with him. I checked with my dad and arranged for Kevin to join the family for a day at Magic Mountain, an amusement park where we were performing.

It was the first time we had seen each other since the Japanese commercials six weeks before. We managed to be alone some by taking walks around the amusement grounds between shows. The attraction I felt for Kevin was more intense than I could have imagined.

Daddy drove us all home that night in the family camper. Kevin and I were sitting in back, almost out of my father's sight but not quite. All the feelings that could be there were, but they had little or no outlet for expression. Kevin's arm around me and his affectionate playing with my hair were innocent enough on the surface, but there was nothing innocent about what was going on inside me.

We rolled into the driveway about 1:00 in the morning. The minute we were all out of the camper, Daddy moved right in to grasp Kevin's hand. "I'm glad we had a chance to get better acquainted. Maybe there will be another chance soon, but it's late now, and I want to get all my girls to bed as quickly as possible. Good night."

"Thanks, Pat. Good night," Kevin said, smiling. I think he found it amusing.

I walked over to where his car was parked, but the area was so brightly lit that even a satisfactory good-night kiss was out of the question. That was the last time I saw him for several months. We spent a lot of time on the phone, trying to scheme ways to get alone together—but to no avail. Sometimes tearfully, sometimes calmly, I kept arguing with my parents.

"Debby, for the last time, no! He's too old, he's not a believer, and I'm your father. You live under my roof, and you'll do as I say."

I began to argue. "You don't understand how I feel."

"You're darned right I don't understand! You're being impossible. You spend one afternoon with the guy, talk a lot on the phone, and then you act like you're having one of the great love affairs of the century. I don't care what you say. That doesn't add up."

There were moments when I knew he was right, that I was creating a fantasy. Kevin was doing the same thing. We had our hearts set on something that couldn't be. Yet, he remained insistent about getting close to me, and I found it difficult to resist encouraging him. It was all very confusing.

Why should a guy like him, with access to hundreds of beautiful girls, get so indignant about not being able to see me? I wondered.

When I asked him that very question, he said it was because I amazed him. He said he was astounded by the kind of person I was and by the strength of my beliefs, like the no-sex thing. He didn't buy any of it, but he was still fascinated.

"Can there really be a girl who thinks that way?" Kevin asked many times.

After many more hassles, my parents asked me to meet with our pastor. I had a good rapport with him and respected his advice, but when he told me how wrong I was, I got defensive.

"I know of other situations where there's a big age difference, even different faiths, and those people have managed to become happily married Christians," I insisted.

But I finally gave up. *What else can I do?* I thought. *My pastor is telling me to stop. My parents are telling me to stop. My sisters think I'm wrong, and. . . .*

Crying at the slightest provocation, I went through the rest of the summer feeling hurt and lonely. Toward fall, Kevin called me from New Mexico, where he was working as part of a movie crew. I was on the road with my family. He wanted me to meet him there, just to leave everything and be with him. It was almost unthinkable, but I was surprised at how seriously I considered his request. I really wanted to go. I'd never felt quite like that before.

Winning a temporary victory in the struggle to control myself, I chose to stay with my family instead of running off to New Mexico. I wrote Kevin and told him I thought it would be best not even to write anymore.

The first night I was home from the tour, the phone rang and Kevin began telling me that my letter was a lot of bull.

"Are you kidding me?" he asked. "Who talked you into such nonsense? Can't you speak for yourself?"

He made it sound like an ultimatum. Did I want to see him or not?

"Yes, but—no . . . you know. . . ." That was all I could say at first. I tried to resist again. "It's wrong. Just leave me alone. Give it up. I'm just getting back on my feet, and I don't want to start. . . ."

"I'm coming over tomorrow, and you can tell me that to my face," he said angrily. He detailed how our relationship was being victimized by outside interference.

Kevin began to convince me. Maybe there was something very deep between us. Maybe it would be impossible to let go of each other.

My parents were very angry when I told them he was coming to see me.

"You may not go anywhere off the premises," my father said. "If you talk, you talk *here*."

That same night a strange thing happened. Albie Pearson, a pastor who is close to our family, visited our home. He'd been out of touch for some time and knew nothing about my relationship with Kevin. Actually, he'd come to pray with my parents about an unrelated problem.

Yet, after dinner, while we were talking and praying, he looked at me and said, "There's a man in your life, isn't there?"

He didn't say "boy" or "guy." He said "man."

"And he's the wrong one," Albie continued. "I know he seems like everything you ever thought you wanted. He's charming, good-looking, funny. . . ."

Kevin's sense of humor was one of the things I liked best about him. He was originally from New York and still had that East Coast wit that always kept me laughing. Albie was describing him perfectly.

As always when people looked me in the eyes and seemed to be figuring out something about me that I didn't want to share, I got uncomfortable, then angry. Albie was especially good at reading me. Sometimes, I wanted to hate him for it.

"You think it can be a perfect relationship," he said, ignoring my cold stare. "But I know the Lord is telling you right now to give it up. It's not for you."

I didn't answer.

Then Albie said, "The Lord wants you to know that, if you do give it up, He has someone right around the corner for you. Someone with more than you ever knew you wanted in a guy."

I couldn't believe what he was saying. Someone must have tipped him off, primed him to work on me.

I turned to my mother. "Did you tell?" Then, to my father, "Did you?"

When they both said "no," I was flabbergasted. I knew they weren't lying.

I'm aware that this incident may seem incredible to some people, but it happened as I've reported it. In the Bible, Paul listed the gifts the Holy Spirit gives to believers. "To one," he wrote, "is given through the Spirit the utterance of wisdom, and to another the utterance of knowledge according to the same Spirit . . ." (1 Corinthians 12:8). This doesn't mean simple human wisdom and knowledge, but something given by the Holy Spirit which could not be had otherwise.

People who exercise these gifts—as Albie did with me when he spoke of Kevin solely on the basis of divine information—can be of real service in the church. I believe, as my church teaches, that what they say should always be examined in the light of the Bible and should never contradict its clear statements. Instead, such information should confirm biblical teaching and serve as a sign to alert the hearer— as it did me—to the intensity of God's involvement in his or her life. In addition, I believe it brings guidance to a specific level seldom available through other means.

The next day dawned sunny and beautiful. Kevin showed up looking great. We went out into the side yard and talked for hours, not just about why I couldn't see him but about everything I believed in. The day lost its magic as he began shooting hard questions at me. All I thought I understood, he tore apart.

Everything I'd heard in church and learned from my parents started sounding foolish. All of a sudden I thought, *How little I really know.* Maybe I'd been believing and living a certain way only because church people and my parents told me that was the thing to do. Maybe it *wasn't* my style. At any rate, I couldn't explain myself, because nothing made sense anymore. The thought that my beliefs might be worthless frightened me terribly.

As we continued talking, he confused me so badly that I just wanted someone to hold me. I'd never been so physically attracted to anyone before. I got an incredible urge to walk right out of the side yard with him, never to come home again. Nearly overwhelmed by temptation, I wanted to say, "Let's go."

The only thing that kept me from it was the fact that Albie Pearson, a person who knew nothing about what was going on, had come the night before and told me that God wanted me to forget Kevin. I couldn't deny that God had *cared,* enough to send someone to help me with a problem I obviously couldn't handle alone.

That's what kept me from leaving everything—my home, my family, my beliefs—behind me in the yard that day.

When I explained my feelings, Kevin insisted that somebody must have told Albie about us ahead of time. But I knew that nobody had; nobody but God. With that one thin shred of faith left, I began arguing that we shouldn't try to keep our relationship going. I told Kevin that I really cared about him, and that I wanted badly not to walk out of his life without having a positive effect on him.

"Actually, I don't want to leave you under any circumstances," I admitted. "But somehow I know I have to. You've gotten me all confused, but one thing I know: There is a God, and He's telling me the best thing to do. In spite of what you say, or what I feel for you, I'm not going to see you anymore."

We walked around to the front of the house. As he was getting into his car, Kevin seemed to change right in front of me.

"Why should you want to be with me?" he asked, with tears in his eyes. "You don't even really know what kind of a guy I am."

He looked at me in a way that I'll never forget. His face seemed to be saying, "Don't you see how awful I am and what I've done to you?" The look told me how sorry he was for what he'd just put me through. He didn't want me to hurt over him. He said he had wanted to hold onto me because he'd seen in me something truly good and a way to change his own life. Maybe that's why he questioned me so intensely. Now he was crying, not because of a desire for me, but because he believed he had lost his chance to make things right for himself.

His desperate, despondent expression devastated me. When he drove away, my entire body ached. As I walked into the house, the pain turned to numbness. I had a feeling that I would never see him again, under any circumstances.

The next day, I went to Canada with the family. I tried to use the time to reevaluate my life, but I couldn't fight off my depression.

Soon after returning to Beverly Hills, I was driving around, doing errands, when I felt a desperate urge to go see Kevin right away. Though I'd never been to his apartment, I knew where it was. I scared myself when I started turning the car in that direction. Fighting back the feeling, I forced myself to go home. I immediately went to my room and stayed there, strangely disturbed for the rest of the day and night. I was asleep the next morning when the maid came to say there was a lady waiting to see me.

"I'll be right down," I said, but something kept me from rushing.

When I did go downstairs, my mother was waiting for me.

"Jenny was mistaken," she said. "The visitor wasn't here to see you. She wanted me."

My mother wouldn't tell me any more. She had a strange look on her face, and during the rest of the day I noticed that she was acting very nervous and mysterious. Cherry had been out jogging when the visitor arrived and had come back just before she left, but she wouldn't say anything either. My mother called my father, who was out of town for the day, and made sure he'd be home the next morning. Then I saw her take Lindy's fiance, Doug, aside and talk to him quietly in a very serious voice.

I asked my other sisters what the big mystery was, but they didn't seem to know. Only then did it cross my mind that something had happened to Kevin. Still, I couldn't get any answers, so I tried to ignore the thought.

After my father got home the next day, he and my mother began calling my sisters up to their bedroom. First Cherry, next Lindy, then, over the intercom, Laury was summoned.

Why am I last all of a sudden? I wondered.

Finally, they called me. I walked into the bedroom and saw them all sitting on the big bed. Everyone was looking at me, their expressions serious.

"What's going on?" I asked Daddy, my voice quaking.

He began with what sounded like a sermon, reminding me that the Lord could give anyone wisdom far beyond what they knew they had.

"Please," I interrupted. "Just tell me."

He went on to explain how the Lord protects us even when the strangest, hardest things happen. Looking back on such situations, we should one day be able to see how God kept them from being a lot worse. He kept on talking, sounding more and more like he was preaching. Then he told me.

"Kevin is dead."

"*I knew it.* I knew it!" I wailed over and over again. "I knew this would happen. Why did it happen?"

For a few minutes, my mother just held me, rocking back and forth while I cried.

"How?" I finally asked, my voice still hysterical.

Daddy tried to calm me while he explained. It had been an accident. "Kevin wasn't feeling well, so he took a pill and had a drink before he went to bed. He died sometime during the night."

I was feeling sick to my stomach, and the rest of my body was numb.

"Why did you wait so long to tell me?"

They had been afraid I'd go to the wake, where the casket was open. My mother wanted to spare me that. At the time, I was angry. I thought I should have been there.

Later, I had a chance to talk with his mother, and she told me that Kevin had always referred to me as his "Snow White." That's when I realized exactly what I had meant to him. He really had wanted to believe that I was right. That's why he had argued so violently with me. I think he had hoped I could convince him to change.

I went through a whole cycle of grief. Hardest to deal with was the feeling that I might have been responsible for his death. I was so confused. I needed time for God to help me understand, from His perspective.

As the months went by, my guilt dissolved, and I began to think of that tumultuous period as one of the most important turning points of my life. It had forced me to reexamine my beliefs. I realized they had to be my own—not just what my parents had taught me. And I knew that I needed to find out more about God and what He was going to mean in my life.

Troubled Children

Now I need to backtrack to the time just before I met Kevin. In June 1974, I graduated, at last, from high school. I had liked Marymount, the school I had eventually switched to, better than any other school I had attended.

My senior year was full of happy times. I was making good grades and was chosen prom queen. But one project absorbed me more than anything else that year. A teacher gave us a term paper assignment. I had read something about autistic children that sparked my interest, so I spent a month researching and wrote my paper on that subject.

Autistic children cut themselves off from the world and live inside their own heads with daydreams and hallucinations. Bruno Bettelheim's *The Empty Fortress* describes the saddest thing about autistic kids. They build up a fortress to protect themselves from the outside world, but they're so young when they start—often only two or three—that the little self inside that fortress is almost nonexistent.

I met Kevin shortly after graduation, and what emotionally seemed such a long relationship, actually covered only that summer. He died in September. I had made no plans for the fall, and my thoughts of Kevin had kept me from thinking much about the future.

Despite the upheaval of those events, I had gotten involved enough with the idea of emotionally disturbed children that

my family heard me talk of little else. Later in the summer
when an acquaintance of my father mentioned that his wife
worked at a school for emotionally disturbed children, it was
natural for Daddy to tell him how interested I was in such
children.

"No kidding," the man replied, raising his eyebrows.
"Hey, why don't you have Debby call my wife? This school
where she works might be able to use her as a volunteer."

"Thanks, I'll do that." I'm sure Daddy smiled when he
thought that he might have stumbled onto something to
occupy me for the next year.

When Daddy made the suggestion later that day, I was
intrigued. The pain of Kevin's death was still pretty intense,
and this sounded like something that would help me think
about it less. I called the woman that evening, and we made
an appointment to meet at the school the following afternoon.

The next day I hopped into my car and headed down the
Ventura Freeway. The woman I had talked with was there at
the school to greet me. She was a lovely lady and took me on
a tour of the entire school. Afterwards, she introduced me to
the gentleman who would determine where my services
could be of most use. I could tell the staff was happy to have
me there, and that I certainly was needed. I was excited.

It all seemed to be working out perfectly until I got home. I
told my parents all about my day and how I couldn't wait to
go back to the school. They both sounded pleased about the
whole thing, but then my mother came up with what she
thought was a brilliant idea.

"Hey, you know, Lindy has just finished a year of college,
and she really doesn't want to start another year right now. It
would be perfect if she volunteered too, and then you two
could be together out there."

"That's a great idea," my dad chimed in.

I didn't want to sound selfish, so I didn't say anything; but
I hated the idea. This was my interest, not Lindy's. All my life
I had had to do everything with my sisters, and I was always

struggling to live up to their achievements. Now I had found something where I could really be on my own, and they wanted to send Lindy along with me.

I tried to give Lindy every out, hoping she really wouldn't be too interested in the plan. But she was, and two days later we were in the car heading for the school.

We were assigned separately as teacher's aides, but first we went through a couple of days of orientation. Most of what they told us was familiar to me from the reading I had done for the term paper.

But some things were new. I watched carefully as they showed us how to subdue a child in a violent fit. The immediate goal was to clasp the child's arms behind his back, wrestle him to the ground, face down, and sit on him until he was calm or until help arrived. The technique looked simple enough, but we didn't get any hand-to-hand training. I was pretty sure it would be harder to do than it looked.

The orientation session also left us with no doubts about the school's view towards religion. Any serious belief in God was regarded as irrelevant and sometimes contrary to the therapeutic process. It was clear, though never said in so many words, that we were not to mention God. I noticed, for example, that the staff went to great lengths to avoid mentioning Christmas. Instead, they were always careful to call it "Winter Holiday."

As we drove home that afternoon, Lindy asked, "Did you get the impression that no one on staff would be too pleased if we talked with the kids about God?"

"Yeah, although I can understand where they're coming from. But I still think it's ridiculous."

"Me, too. I guess, though, if we don't want to get kicked out, we'd better be careful about what we say."

"Well, let's just trust the Lord to give us the opportunities and show us how to use them."

"Sounds good to me."

Our volunteer commitment was for two to three days each week. That first week we worked Monday, Wednesday, and

Friday. I was assigned to a classroom of about a dozen children who ranged in age from eight to twelve. The school had grouped them together, in spite of age differences, because generally they had the same level of academic skills and achievement. However, these kids were not able to work together as do children in a regular classroom. Instead, we basically had to tutor them individually.

Two teachers were in charge of this class. They were both young men, probably in their late twenties. Frank was stockily built, fair-haired, and casually but conservatively dressed. Scott was an angular guy, tall with long black hair and a moustache. He was customarily unkempt next to Frank and more "laid back." The two of them made an interesting pair. After opening day preliminaries and various get-acquainted activities, we launched into the business at hand: teaching reading and math to children whose emotional problems often got in the way of the learning process.

The teacher-student ratio was one to four, but even at that, the struggle to maintain order was constant. Often one of the kids, frustrated by some problem, would leap to his feet and run around the room in a screaming fit. This, in turn, would upset the others, so that Frank, Scott, and I would have our hands full. Usually whoever was closest to the child at the moment would try to catch him. Meanwhile, the other two of us would instantly drop whatever we were doing and position ourselves on the alert, to prohibit any of the other kids from taking the opportunity to cause some further disturbance.

Early on, I was drawn to one child in particular. His name was David, and he was nine years old. David talked a lot about God. Gradually, as I listened, I pieced together a picture of how David saw himself. In that picture, God was standing just behind him, watching him closely on behalf of David's father. And this God was instantly furious whenever David couldn't measure up in the classroom.

I had read that when children are quite young, they perceive their parents as god-like—omnipresent, omniscient, all-powerful. For most of us, it takes a while for this perception to be modified. But for David, it wasn't being modified at all. God was a distinct person from his father in David's thinking, but in one very real sense they were one and the same. God was the spirit of his father's harshness and disapproval, who accompanied David wherever he went.

In a way, I knew how David felt, but I also knew his picture of God was terribly wrong. However, I couldn't talk to David about this in the classroom. Frank and Scott would have told me I was aggravating David's problem.

I had a different opinion. David, I was certain, needed God's help to overcome his insecurities and emotional problems. It was essential that he discover what God the Father is really like. I yearned to help him do that, and I prayed earnestly for an opportunity.

In a way, I had already been laying the groundwork. Lindy and I both made a habit of praying silently for the children whenever we had opportunity to touch them. (By now, I didn't resent Lindy's presence at the school nearly so much!) In the normal course of our work, we were often bending over their desks to help them with one problem or another. It was quite natural at those times to rest a hand on their shoulder and thus establish a point of contact. The Bible mentions prayer accompanied by the laying on of hands as an instrument of healing. Touching the students was a way of expressing love and also served as a point of contact for conveying God's grace and healing power.

I had been doing that pretty steadily with David for several weeks. One day, as I was working with him, he became extremely agitated and began to yell, "David, you're so stupid! God probably hates you because you're so dumb."

Frank hurried over. "Debby, why don't you take David out into the hallway for a few minutes? Give him a chance to calm down."

"Okay." I always enjoyed taking kids into the hallway,

because it was my only chance to be alone with them. The rule was that a trained professional must always be near at hand. This didn't violate that rule, and yet it gave me the opportunity to speak privately with the child.

Out in the hallway, I crouched down so I could look into David's eyes. For a moment, I just held him in my arms, praying silently that the Holy Spirit would help him calm down. In a few moments, I began to feel the tension leaving. I pulled back and looked at him with a big smile.

"Feeling better?" I asked.

"A little bit." His expression was bewildered.

"Do you know why you feel better?"

"No."

"Because when I was holding you, I was asking God to help you."

David stiffened. "God hates me. My dad told me He does!"

"That's not true." I crooked my forefinger under his chin and pulled until our eyes met. "God isn't like that. He loves you all the time. He loves you when you do good things, and He still loves you when you make mistakes with your math. He would never call you stupid. He wants to help you grow up to be a good and happy person."

David didn't say anything. But I could tell by the intense expression in his eyes that he was probing my face to detect any insincerity or falsehood. What I was saying challenged everything in him—it was utterly foreign and strange. Yet it also spoke of love, acceptance, and freedom. It might be, he feared, too good to be true.

"David," I went on, my hands resting on his little shoulders, "right now I'm asking God just to hold you in His arms and hug you. You know that nice feeling inside? That's God showing you that He loves you. Now, let's go back inside and get to work on that arithmetic problem. Oh, and this little talk we've had will be our secret," I added, hoping he wouldn't go straight to a staff member and repeat what I had said.

That evening, on the way home, I excitedly told Lindy what had happened with David. It marked a breakthrough, and both of us were really glad. After a while, Lindy grew pensive.

"You know," she began, "I've really had to face up to some things, watching these kids. The ones I've gotten to know have been raised in homes where discipline is either hit-and-miss or nonexistent."

"I know what you're going to say," I interrupted. "And I hate to admit it, but I'm beginning to agree. I still think Dad and Mom were overprotective with us, but I have to say that I can see some good in the way they set boundaries and really enforced them."

"Yeah, have you seen it? Most of the time, when one of the kids starts having a fit, he's really asking someone to give order and direction to his life," Lindy said.

"Even if it means having someone sit on him," I added.

"Remember how Daddy used to tell us we were just asking for a spanking?"

"Yeah, I guess we were, too—sometimes."

Spankings, however, were not part of the program at the school. Instead, the staff had two major procedures for controlling the children's behavior—in addition, that is, to wrestling them to the ground and sitting on them. One was drugs, prescribed by psychiatrists to eliminate any chemical imbalance there might be; the other was a system of rewards. The children earned points for good behavior. They could then exchange those points for whatever they wanted at a little store in each classroom. Candy was the inevitable choice.

By the standards that governed the school, spankings were regarded as detrimental. *But are they really?* I wondered. *Are drugs and sugar a better way to handle behavioral problems?*

Probably I was oversimplifying things. I'm certainly no expert in psychotherapy. But I know there are some experts who question drug therapy. From both reading and personal experience, I'm convinced that too much refined sugar is nearly poisonous by almost any standards.

One day, I was helping to supervise the playground. One

little boy named Joey refused to go back to the classroom after recess. Frank went off with the rest of the class and left me with the chore of convincing Joey to come along.

I walked to the slide. "C'mon, Joey, time to go."

"Okay, Debby. Just one more time," he said as he started to climb the metal steps.

"No, Joey. Not one more time. We need to go now."

He ignored me and continued climbing. I took him by the arm, led him down the steps, and started off toward the classroom. Suddenly he erupted in a violent fit. He thrashed about and kicked wildly. I held onto his wrist for dear life and tried to follow through with the restraining techniques I'd been taught, but to no avail. I couldn't get a grip on him. In the meantime, my shins came within range of his cowboy boots. He kicked my right leg with two glancing blows; then, all of a sudden, he landed a brutal jab squarely in the middle of my left shin. Then came another and another.

With that I gave up the fight. I released my grip on his wrist and just sat on the ground, crying softly. It was completely unprofessional and Joey had won, but all I knew at that moment was that my legs hurt terribly. I also felt embarrassed at my failure. But then, the strangest thing happened. I wiped my eyes and looked up to see little Joey gazing down at me with concern.

My collapse had totally disarmed him. "Are you okay?" Joey asked.

"No, I'm not okay," I said. "You *hurt* me with your kicking. Why would you do that?"

"I didn't mean to hurt you, but I got so angry."

"Joey, it's okay to be angry, but it's not okay to kick people and hurt them because of it. I understand that you didn't want to come inside, but there's a time for play and a time for work. You'll get another chance to play later."

"Okay. I'm so sorry I hurt you. I didn't mean to, really."

"I know, Joey. It's okay. I'll be all right. Let's go."

He took my hand and followed me like a little puppy back to the classroom. I never told Frank or Scott what had happened. They must have wondered, though, because Joey fretted about me all afternoon. He was extra friendly, cuddling up to me whenever he could, holding my hand. He was the littlest kid in the class and had a reputation as a fighter. But that afternoon he was the sweetest child of all.

I don't pretend to understand fully what happened that day, but somehow my honest response to Joey's outburst had caused him to see that other people, people he cared about, could be hurt by his negative behavior. Maybe in that instance, if he had been physically pinned to the ground, isolated in a hallway, and had points taken away, his anger would have been reinforced. Instead, Joey was truly sorry for what he had done, and I never had another moment of trouble with him.

The ten months Lindy and I spent at the school were seldom uneventful and never boring. I did find myself chafing under the rules, which forbade me to exercise much responsibility. As I grew in experience, I wanted to do more and more.

Toward the end of my volunteer year, Frank and Scott decided to allow me to teach the class for an hour one day. I had made a suggestion that it might be interesting to look up the meaning of each child's name, translating the meaning into a goal for each child to live up to. I'm not sure if Frank really liked the idea or if he just wanted to pacify my desire for greater responsibility, but I was pleased nonetheless when he asked me to prepare the lesson and teach it the following week.

I was particularly excited because I really felt the Lord had given me this idea. It's obvious throughout the Bible that the Lord considers names to be very important. Oftentimes, the words appear, "And he shall be called . . ." when the Lord was specifically directing a mother in how to name her child. Other times, the Lord would alter a person's name to denote a special calling for his life. For example, *Abram* ("exalted father") was changed to *Abraham* ("father of a multitude"), foretelling that he would become the father of a new nation.

One of the most poignant examples is that of John the Baptist, whose name means "Jehovah hath been gracious." The phrase referred not only to his mother Elizabeth's old age and former barrenness but also to John's ministry of making the transition from law to grace.

As I began my research, I was delighted to see that David's name means "beloved." I had had many opportunities since that first time in the hall to tell him about how much God loved him. Slowly, he was coming to believe it. The discovery of the meaning of his name would be, I was certain, a real boost to him.

David's name was the first on the list as I began the lesson.

"Okay, let's start with you, David. Do you have any idea what your name means?"

Feeling very excited about the whole situation, David got a little silly and answered, "Yeah. Tuna!" and burst into laughter, taking the entire class with him. "Tuna" was a favorite word with the kids. They used it as slang for excrement. Frank and Scott watched me closely to see if I could handle the outburst.

Under my breath, I whispered, "Lord, help me keep things in control. . . ."

"David, now pay close attention, because I really think you're going to like what your name means!"

The class quieted right down, and David waited attentively to hear the real meaning.

"Your name, David, means 'beloved.' Do you know what that means?"

"Kind of," he said with a smile.

"Well, in the dictionary it says that 'beloved' means 'loved; greatly loved; and dear to the heart.'

"Now, David, I want you to think about two things concerning your name. First, I want you to think about the times when you get frustrated and you can't do something the way you want to, and you convince yourself that Frank or Scott or your parents or God or someone hates you because of it. You know how you do that?"

David nodded shyly.

"Well, from now on I want you to think about your name at times like that and remember that we all love you and want to help you. Okay?"

"Okay!" David was beaming.

"And next, I want you to start thinking of ways you can help other people and show your love for them as a way of living up to your name. Does that sound like a good goal for you?"

"Sure. You mean like helping Frank and Scott clean things up in the classroom . . . or helping Lucky calm down when he gets too upset and things like that?"

"That's exactly what I mean. And you know, not only will that help people to like you more, but it will also make you feel really good about yourself."

David sat back smiling, his mind spinning with new ideas for living up to his name, and I continued with what turned out to be a very successful lesson.

Joseph, it turned out, meant "increaser." What could have been better for the shortest kid in the class? Little Joey was fascinated.

The meaning of Frank's name, I learned, came from medieval days. In Old English, *franka* meant "spear" or "javelin." Today it retains some of that meaning. When we say that someone speaks frankly, we mean he gets right to the point and doesn't mince words. Our Frank was a straightforward sort of person. It fit and he obviously liked it.

Scott's name drew our attention to Scotland and its heritage of bravery, piety, fierce independence, and thrift. The expression "scot-free" stems, so says the dictionary, from Old English *gescot*, which means "payment."

Deborah means "bee" or "wasp" in Hebrew. I used that to make a couple of jokes about myself. But I also told the kids how I'd seen that bees only sting when provoked. They really spend most of their time making honey, something we all enjoy.

"You did a good job today." There was sincerity in Frank's

voice as we were cleaning up after class that day. "The kids loved it."

"Thanks very much," I replied, equally sincere.

"You know, I'd never given the meanings of names much attention. I guess I was dimly aware that they had meanings, but. . . ."

"Yeah, I know what you mean. I really had fun looking them up. It was new to me, too."

"It was amazing how the meaning of every kid's name tied into his or her problem and had something to do with overcoming that problem. It took a little ingenuity to come up with that every time," Frank said.

"Thanks." I blushed. I loved the commendation. It felt good for a special reason: I loved the children. From the start we had hit it off famously. They regularly flocked around me when I arrived at school, and there was plenty of loving and hugging. Still, Frank and Scott were compelled to enforce all the professional rules which always seemed to restrict how much I could work with the kids. That's why I felt especially good when they relaxed the rules enough to let me take charge of the class for even an hour.

June 1975 was a marked contrast to June of '74. Toward the end of May, some staff members called Lindy and me aside before we left one afternoon.

"At our staff meeting the other morning, all of us got to talking about how we've enjoyed the volunteer work you two have done this year. We decided to throw a little thank-you party on the last day of school. Can you be there?"

"Of course, we'll be there!" we said. Lindy and I were the only volunteers that year. We thought it was pretty special for them to go to that much trouble for just the two of us.

The last day, after kissing and hugging every kid goodbye, I walked across the little compound to a house on campus where one of the staff couples lived. They had prepared some refreshments. One of the teachers brought a guitar and entertained us with some songs he'd written. It was a happy time and a really nice way to be told "thank you."

Lindy and I finally drove away late in the afternoon. We didn't talk much, both of us silently reviewing experiences of the past several months. The job had been hard work, but the experience had been good. To drive off like that, only saying goodbye, wasn't easy. I hoped I would get the chance to work and spend time with children again—especially with troubled children.

Gabri

When my year as a volunteer ended, one of the few things I looked forward to was a Monday night Bible study that was conducted in our home. Our pastor, Jack Hayford, led it. He had a way of teaching the Bible so that we felt God was talking to us intimately about our immediate situation.

One night, my friends, Maria Ferrer and her brother, Miguel, came to the study as usual. But that night, they brought along another member of their family, their brother Gabriel.

I had met Gabriel only once before, on Easter Sunday, 1974. I had recently broken up with Brian and had been dating Gabri's older brother Miguel for a little while. Miguel had been with me at Marymount's traditional all night graduation party (well-chaperoned, of course!), and we had decided to stay up and go to the Easter sunrise service at the Church on the Way. We stopped by Miguel's house to ask Gabri, who was interested neither in church nor in Christianity, to come along. When we flipped on the lights in Gabri's room, I could see immediately that Gabri was a long way from joining us. He bolted straight up in bed, hair falling well past his shoulders, glared at us with a menacing look, and in a restrained, even voice said, "It is 6:30 in the morning." I backed out of the room and didn't see him again for nearly a year.

During that year, Gabri, surprisingly enough, became a Christian. So, on this evening at the Bible study, we "re-met" and began talking, mostly about tennis. He suggested that we practice together, since we both confessed to being less than adequate players. My answer was unintentionally non-committal: "If I can find the time." Gabri laughed and replied, "Okay, I can take a hint."

I quickly explained that I really *was* busy, traveling with the family doing concerts, but I also wanted to get together and play. The following week at the same Bible study, we made a tennis date. It was the first of many. Gabri didn't have much money to spend, and Daddy was still strict about where I went on a date. Our courtship was conducted mainly on tennis courts and at Bible studies, both of which were inexpensive and enjoyable ways to spend time.

I couldn't remember being with anyone before who had made me laugh so much. We shared wide-ranging senses of humor, and I guess that common trait helped to draw us closer together. Even our relationship had its share of humor. Our first kiss is a good example.

Certainly, most couples remember their first kiss. But how many would think it was funny if they'd had to wait six months before anything happened?

It was a warm summer's night when Gabri finally put his arms around me. *This is it,* I thought. I closed my eyes in anticipation. A moment later, I discovered I'd closed them too soon. Gabri only meant to kiss me on the forehead. I ended up kissing the air under his chin, making a loud smacking sound and my face turning bright red. I was horrified as I drove home, hoping that by some miracle Gabri hadn't noticed.

My best friend, Donna Freberg, also happened to be a close friend of Gabri's—for a long while, in fact, before I'd ever met him. From the start of my relationship with Gabri, I confided in her often about how things were going between us. We rolled on the floor laughing when I told her about my misplaced kiss.

"Every time we go out together, I think maybe he's finally going to kiss me, but he never does," I complained.

Donna promised to talk to Gabri about it. After seeing him, she reported back to me that the main problem was that he was scared to death. I was the first Christian girl he had ever dated. He wasn't quite sure how to act or what was the proper thing to do. After Donna assured him that I would not slap his face and run off crying if he tried to kiss me, our relationship developed gradually and naturally.

That summer of 1975 we spent getting better acquainted. Gabri had graduated from school now, too, but neither of us had clearly defined plans for our futures.

I attended my family's church on Sunday mornings and went with Gabri to a new church, called the Vineyard, on Sunday afternoons. The pastor's name was Kenn Gulliksen. We got into the habit of attending a home meeting in our area which Kenn led on Friday nights.

As the summer pressed on toward autumn, I became increasingly concerned about my lack of plans. What was I supposed to do? I was sure God had plans for me, but I had no idea what they involved for the coming months. I prayed a lot but was still undecided. Finally, in mid-August, I decided to go on a fast. The next morning, Friday, I skipped breakfast. The occasional complaints from my stomach reminded me to keep believing God for guidance.

I was still praying and fasting when time for Bible study came. Gabri was out of town, visiting his dad, who was appearing in a play in Sacramento, so I went alone. At the meeting, I was talking with one of the other girls when Kenn Gulliksen walked over.

"Hi," he greeted us. "Excuse me, Debby. I wanted to get these materials about our Bible school into Gabri's hands. Would you give them to him when he gets back?"

"Okay. He gets back tomorrow, and I'll make sure he gets them."

"Great. Tell him if he's interested, he'd better sign up soon."

I smiled as I leafed through the material. Gabri had said a couple of things that told me he was reluctant to dive right into another year of school. I was looking at the syllabus of courses when a light went on in my head. I knew this was it; the answer to my prayer.

When I got home, I began to rationalize. *Those papers don't necessarily mean anything to me. They're for Gabri. Kenn didn't suggest I look them over and see if I was interested. If the Lord was really trying to tell me to go, Kenn should have said something to me.*

I went back and forth with myself. I felt a strange excitement about the prospect, but like Gabri, I was hesitant about committing myself to a regular schedule with homework and tests. A year had gone by since I had been in school, and I was not at all sure I wanted to go back.

Saturday afternoon, I drove the few blocks to Gabri's house. We had a date to play tennis. He lived in a little guest house connected to the garage. I knocked.

"Hi," he greeted me as he opened the door. It was good to see him.

"How was your dad?" I asked.

"Fine." He talked for a while about the trip.

"Gabri, Kenn Gulliksen gave me these last night. And I've had the strangest feeling about them. . . ." I recited the details of the argument I'd been having with myself as we walked over to the court. After a couple of sets, we sat down to rest on a bench.

"What do you think?" I asked. "Should I go?"

"Well, I know how you feel. I just graduated less than two months ago and I sure hadn't planned to go back to school this soon. But this Bible school idea is intriguing."

We looked at each other and grinned.

"I think we're going," I said.

"I do, too, but I don't believe it."

We both laughed. Neither of us had any idea what we were getting ourselves into, but we knew it was right. And it was nice to think that it would give us five or six hours a day together.

A few weeks later, the semester opened. Classes started each morning at 7:30. So, that first night I set the alarm for 6:45. When it went off the next morning, Monday, I rolled out of bed, threw some water on my face, jumped into jeans, sweatshirt, and tennis shoes, downed some juice, and was soon on the road to pick up Gabri.

"Good morning," I said with a yawn as he climbed into the car.

"Good morning," he groaned. "I can't believe I'm actually out on the street moving at this hour. Thanks for picking me up."

"Don't worry about it. I don't mind driving. What's the schedule today?"

"The way I understand it, first hour is Greek, then hermeneutics, the Book of Genesis and, finally, discipleship. Everything's over at 1:00."

"Explain to me again what hermeneutics is or are?"

"It's the study of the principles of interpretation—in this case, the interpretation of the Bible. The word comes from Greek mythology. Hermes, or as he was known to the Romans, Mercury, was the winged messenger of the gods on Mt. Olympus. He carried and interpreted the messages of Zeus and the others to mere mortal men."

"You know, you could probably win a trivia contest with boring stuff like that."

"I know. I looked it up last night."

Actually, our first day was devoted to orientation. Only this was a different kind of orientation. Kenn explained that he and the other teachers believed that God had assembled us all there.

"The main thing we want to do this morning is to take time to gather around each of you, one at a time, and pray for you. As we do, we're going to ask the Lord for His special will to be clear for each one."

I watched as they prayed over others. My turn came in about the middle of the group. Kenn's hand rested lightly on my head, while one of the teachers asked God to fill me with His grace. Then there was a moment of silence.

"Debby," Kenn said, "as I pray over you one passage in the Bible stands out in my mind. It is 'Christ in you, the hope of glory.' It's in this, I believe, you'll find the answer to your frustrations."

I quietly thanked God for this encouragement as the staff passed on to the next student.

His word about my frustrations made me think. I *had* felt frustrated in the last several months. The year working with kids had been good. Now the prospect of Bible school was exciting. But neither of these was really what I wanted to do for my whole life. Where was I headed?

Deep in my heart the thing I loved most was singing and entertaining. That was a life that offered glory—a fleeting sort at best. The only true source of glory—and it was quite another kind from what the entertainment world had to offer—was Christ in me. I rested in that and, as I did, I realized more strongly than ever that I was where God wanted me.

Gabri was the last in line for prayer, and I was especially eager to hear what they would say to him. When his turn came, I listened intently. But, there was no message for him. And they didn't try to contrive something just so he'd be like all the rest of us. Instead, they let that silence be his message.

For a moment, that was bewildering to me. But, the more I thought about it, the more I felt it signified something special—and good—that God would reveal in time.

The next day, classes began in earnest. Gabri and I settled into our chairs for the first hour. There were about fifteen of us assembled behind three or four tables. Larry Meyers, our Greek teacher, walked in, greeted us, and passed out our textbook, a little hardcover edition by a man with the stuffy name of J. Gresham Machen. By the time he covered the alphabet and started talking about conjugating a little word called *luo*, I was lost. That night, I sat down to what was to

become the long and gruesome task of learning to conjugate
luo through the various moods, tenses, and voices of New
Testament Greek—the language spoken throughout the Ro-
man Empire at the time of Christ. To study it was a real
exercise of the will.

But I'm getting ahead of myself. With the end of that first
day came a bigger challenge than Greek verbs. Kenn Gulliksen was teaching our class in the principles of discipleship.

"We want to maintain a good emphasis on study here, but
the primary purpose of the school is not to make scholars out
of you. We agree with Paul in his first letter to Timothy when
he said, 'Now the end of the commandment is charity out of a
pure heart, and of a good conscience, and of faith unfeigned'
[KJV]. The purpose of this class is to focus on what that
means in terms of our day-to-day lifestyles and of our lifetime
goals.

"Open your Bibles to the book of Exodus, chapter twenty-
three, starting with verse nineteen: 'The first of the first fruits
of your ground you shall bring into the house of the LORD
your God.' I think there are a number of ways in which we
could apply this principle in our own lives, but the one I want
to talk to you about today is the way of a morning devotion."

I gulped.

"Giving God that very first part of your day in Bible reading and prayer honors Him in a special way, and it also re-
leases power in our lives that won't otherwise be there. David
spoke of his morning prayers and sacrifices to God in the fifth
and sixty-third Psalms. . . ."

Kenn went on to speak of Jesus' rising early for prayer. He
also told us that it was the custom of nearly every significant
Christian leader of whom he had read. He cited people like
Hudson Taylor, Andrew Murray, and John Wesley, who
attributed much of their success to the practice of giving God
the firstfruits of their time each day.

I had heard this sort of thing off and on for years, not least
of all from my parents. It was one of those things, I was
convinced, that everybody applauded but few people actu-

ally practiced. Anyway, it seemed to me that another time of day would be as suitable, if not more—then I could read and pray in a more wakeful state than I could at dawn.

"Whether or not you're convinced this is a good idea, I want you to start doing it anyway," Kenn continued, "much as if it were a homework assignment from this class. This is not optional while you're in this school. And I want you to start keeping a prayer notebook—logging requests and answers to prayer, as well as insights the Lord gives you during your quiet times."

This was getting to be a bit much. Some familiar and unpleasant feelings began to rise in me. An authority figure was telling me I *had* to do something.

But Kenn didn't hear my silent cries of protest.

"Set your alarm tomorrow morning for a half hour earlier than usual. Get out of bed and find a place where you're comfortable, but awake. I use a chair by the window. Have your Bible and your prayer notebook laid out and ready to go. Get before the Lord, and spend a few minutes just worshipping Him and offering up a morning sacrifice of praise. Sing some songs to Him; it doesn't have to be loud. Ask Him to help you hear His voice as you open the Bible and read at least two or three chapters.

"Then open your prayer notebook. Make a special note always to ask for guidance and protection for the day ahead. Ask Him to bless our nation and its leaders, the church and its leaders, and then go on to your personal prayer requests. Keep a list of those you pray for. Then I want you to do one last thing. Spend some time being quiet before the Lord, to allow Him to speak to you.

"I think you'll be surprised how quickly that half hour goes by when you approach it like this."

I did not want to do it. On the way home that afternoon, I proceeded to list my objections to Gabri. "This is too legalistic and confining. Even if it is a homework assignment, I ought to be given some choice about when I'm going to do it. I don't think it's fair!"

Gabri nodded thoughtfully. "I guess I just see it as a discipline—part of what it means to go to this school. Though how I'm ever going to wake up that early is a mystery to me."

I smiled—remembering that first time I'd met Gabri and how his brother and I had interrupted his sleep. He was certainly better-natured about it now than he was that day. I decided to resign myself to the idea, at least for the present.

The next morning my radio alarm went off at 6:15. I had gotten to bed the night before by 11:00 so it wasn't too horrible. Still, it took me a couple of minutes to get my head together, get out of bed, and get ready in front of my open Bible. What transpired in the next twenty-five minutes was pretty much according to the outline Kenn had given us. At the end I felt as though I had fulfilled a duty. It had not been particularly exhilarating. Nothing special had happened—except that I had obeyed.

I still wasn't convinced about how worthwhile this early rising devotional program really was. I argued about it with Kenn, Gabri, myself, and, I suppose, God for the next several days. But, each morning, I got up at 6:15 and did it.

The next week however, I started to notice a new pattern developing. Instead of my days aligning themselves in a haphazard fashion, it was as if they unfolded before me. If there were any unexpected snags or problems, I would find answers often as soon as they were sought. I found Proverbs 3:6 coming true. "In all your ways acknowledge him, and he will make straight your paths."

As with most of God's principles, what had looked like a restrictive cage, once I stepped into it, turned into a pair of wings—true freedom.

Life with my parents still felt like a cage, however. One day, after my last class, I found myself discussing that relationship with Kenn. He was well aware of my frustrations.

"How's it been going between you and your folks?" he asked.

"I guess it's getting better, but it's slow."

"Sounds okay. These things seldom happen overnight."
I sighed.

"By the way, how does Gabri like having to have you home by 11:00?"

"Oh, he's great about it. I never feel any pressure from him about that. That's probably one of the reasons things have gotten quieter. They like him and he likes them—and doesn't object to their rules—and I don't get caught in the middle."

"Praise the Lord for that!"

"I do. Actually, an entirely different problem frustrates me these days."

"What's that?"

"Well, I've been pretty sure for several years now that I'm supposed to be a singer and an entertainer. And recently a number of people have been urging me to launch out and give it a try."

"Like who?"

"Well, Mike Curb, for one. I was talking with him just a few days ago. He was telling me he thinks I've got the talent to make it. He's eager for me to cut a single and to help me get started."

"I see. Well, Mike certainly knows the record business. What do your parents say?"

"No."

"Just like that—no?"

"Oh, they keep talking about God's timing and my maturity, but it always ends up as no."

"Do you think they're trying to hold you down just for the sake of exercising their authority?"

"I suppose not, but how long do I have to wait?"

"Debby, I'll be straight with you. I think how long you have to wait depends mostly on you."

"What do you mean?"

"The Bible's clear on the subject. God gave you parents as those to whom He's delegated His authority. When you choose to submit to them, you choose the path of freedom.

The principle's not at all unlike what you went through with those early morning devotions. By bringing yourself into subjection, you set yourself free."

"But that doesn't make it easy."

"I'll grant you that—but don't settle for less. You've got a head start because your folks have been believers for a long time. You're still new at hearing the Lord's voice. Why not let them take the responsibility for these heavy decisions. God knows you won't be able to enjoy *that* luxury much longer."

"I've never thought of it as a luxury before."

"Don't worry, you will."

Kenn kept encouraging me to see my parents from a biblical perspective. I knew he was right, but somehow, in the nitty-gritty of daily life, knowing truth in my head came a lot more easily and quickly than living it in my actions.

But if I felt that my professional career was not zooming ahead according to my schedule, the Vineyard School more than made up for it. I count those days as among the most valuable I have ever spent. I was getting grounded in what I believed, and *why*. I was challenging ideas I had always automatically accepted, thinking things through in light of what the Bible says, and either confirming or altering my perspective on the subject. During this year my beliefs became my way of life, instead of only a part of life. More important, my belief in Jesus as the Son of God grew into a very personal and intimate relationship.

Another factor that helped me mature spiritually that year was spending a lot of time with people with whom I could relate on many levels of life. Often, before, I had felt isolated. Churchgoers were people with whom I had little else in common. With my new classmates, however, I found a group who shared not only my love for God but also interests, goals, and backgrounds that were like mine. We enjoyed a closeness and camaraderie I had seldom felt before.

One experience, though, is a very sore spot in my memories of the year. Each student was assigned a chapter in the Book of Romans to read dramatically before the class. The teacher intended to motivate us first to study the given chapter in depth and then to try to communicate the meaning to the rest of the class.

To get up in front of fourteen other people and give a dramatic reading, even if it was from the Bible, was petrifying. I had barely gotten used to singing alone (and then only in church or before small groups) much less to giving an acting demonstration. For weeks before my turn came, I whined about not understanding the purpose of the exercise—hoping I might thereby get out of the requirement. No such luck.

On the day of my reading, another student went first. Anticipating my own performance, I held my breath and prayed for him to do well. Even though several in the class were professional performers, he appeared relaxed. Taking his part quite seriously, he actually introduced himself as Paul the apostle and shook hands with one of the students. The whole class exploded in laughter. *Almost* the whole class; I was livid. Afraid they'd make fun of my reading too, I stood up and screamed, *"What is so funny? If everyone is going to take this so lightly, I'm not going to take part in it!"*

There was a stunned silence. I sat back down in my chair, ready to cry. Everyone's eyes were on me as the student slowly continued the reading. Soon my turn came and, somehow, I got through my chapter. Everyone was very supportive. Of course, after my previous outburst, I doubt they would have dared to be otherwise.

I began to thrive on my expanding knowledge of Christianity. At the same time, I was feeling wonderful about my relationship with Gabri. Always together or talking on the phone for hours, never wanting to say good night, we were inseparably in love. A day hardly went by that I didn't thank the Lord for putting us together.

One day in late October, as I was praying, I felt an uneasiness inside. I had come to recognize that feeling as God's way of letting me know something was wrong. I knew the "something" was Gabri and me. I tried to ignore the signal, but for more than a week my prayers seemed to bounce off the ceiling. Finally I asked the Lord what specifically was wrong. It was then I realized that God was asking me to give up Gabri. Our relationship was not to continue, at least not in the same way that it had.

I could not understand. I was in love with Gabri, happy to have a relationship without hassles. The defenses I usually raised with guys were coming down. Although I was beginning to respond to Gabri in many ways, our physical desires were very much under control. Actually, we seemed more spiritually-minded than I'd ever imagined men and women could be together. What fault could God possibly find with our relationship?

I tried so hard to understand. Maybe, as when God asked Abraham to sacrifice His son Isaac, I was being asked to demonstrate my faith. Didn't that mean I'd only have to give up Gabri for a little while? Wasn't God merciful? Hadn't he spared Isaac as soon as his father laid him on the altar and took the knife in hand? If all I had to do was prove. . . . No, I knew my thinking was wrong. I couldn't tag a condition onto this obedience. I had to let go of Gabri with no expectation of getting together again.

When I finally told Gabri that we had to break up, I cried and said, "I would never do this if I didn't feel it was God's will."

Tears filled Gabri's eyes, too. Then he told me that, if I really thought separating was God's will, I should go with it.

I kept praying, but the answer was always the same. We broke off our relationship. Immediately afterward, I began to feel peaceful. I didn't understand all the reasons, but I knew I had done the right thing.

Six weeks before the breakup, Gabri had given me his gold baby ring for my nineteenth birthday. His initials were its only ornamentation. I wore the little ring constantly. He loved to see it on my finger. As I was beginning to accept the end of our romance, I felt God asking me to take the ring off and return it to Gabri. Heartbroken, I stayed in my room and argued with God.

Later I wrote a letter:

November 5, 1975

To Gabri, whom I shall always love,

If it were not for the grace and mercy of our Lord and Shepherd, this letter would be the cruelest thing I could ever give you. If I were not sure beyond a shadow of a doubt that His love was sufficient for you, I would never be able to deliver this. Please know that.

I went home today feeling better about our situation and full of hopes and expectations because of how obviously the Lord had begun sustaining and working in us. I went upstairs and sat on my bed to think and to thank God for the bit of relief I felt. Almost instantly, the words came to me. "Now, take off your ring." Very quickly I began to think of all the reasons that God couldn't possibly require that of me, too. Some of my reasons were:

"I still love Gabri and just because I wear his ring doesn't mean I haven't done what God asked."

"It's too final . . . too extreme . . . too hard."

"It will be too painful for me to do that to Gabri. He's hurting enough. Don't make me do that, too."

God gently, but painfully, told me that with those reasons I had clearly shown Him that I had not given my hopes and expectations to Him. I was not relying on Him totally for strength and, most of all, I still carried a heavy burden for you.

Gabri, I don't think I've ever wanted to die more in my whole life than right then. I cried out to God, and again He spoke to me. God said that in taking off the ring, I could really place on the altar all my hopes and expectations that He would restore our relationship. It would be a symbol of my total dependence on Him and, most important to me, it would free God to supply the love and strength you need right now.

You know, as I took that ring off, I really felt human love being torn out of every part of my being. Then I realized that God was not being cruel. A supernatural love replaced what I was losing.

I know how badly this hurts you, and I know you are crying now as you read this. It is the hardest thing I have ever done in my life, Gabri, but I know with all my heart that God loves us beyond all our understanding. I know He will fill the emptiness we feel piercing through us now.

I love you in a way I have never known before,
Debby

Later that night, I went over to Gabri's and left the letter and the ring on the bed in his empty room.

I didn't see Gabri again until a week later. He kept an appointment to play the piano while I sang on a TV program. The experience of being together was like walking a tightrope. Balancing my still deep feelings for Gabri with my commitment to God was difficult.

The next time I saw Gabri, his attitude was cooler. Asking why we should keep hurting ourselves, he suggested making a clean break. I agreed wholeheartedly, but it never seemed to come to that. Somehow our lives kept crossing, not to mention the fact that we were still in school together every day. We would try not to speak to each other for a week, then slowly gravitate back into each other's life. We would start getting too emotionally involved and feel uneasy about it. So we would swing back the other way and try to have nothing to do with each other again. It was a maddening cycle, and at times I felt as if God was taunting us—playing a sadistic game with two hearts. It took us about a year to realize that what *He* wanted to do was to advance the friendship level of our relationship, keeping the romantic element dormant. Slowly, God was building our individual lives together in a way we could have never engineered ourselves.

The Last Spanking

After the end of the Vineyard Bible School in the spring, our family started a tour of one-nighters which ended at the Ohio State Fair. The last show was marked with a tinge of melancholy. The chances were unlikely we'd be performing again as a family, since Lindy and Cherry were both soon to be married.

After we said goodbye to our musicians and staff with many hugs and a few tears, my sisters and I trudged back to the hotel. Mom and Dad weren't there yet, still at the fairgrounds finishing up business. It was late, but I was hungry. I knew the hotel restaurant and coffee shop were closed, so I decided to get something out of the vending machine in the hallway. As I headed out the door, I neglected to say where I was going and just told the others I'd be back in a minute.

Out in the hallway, I changed my mind and took the elevator down to the lobby. There were more food machines on the first floor. I stepped out of the elevator, and there was our drummer, Bobby. He and I had developed a close friendship over the years that he had worked for the family.

"Hi, Bobby."

"Hi."

"You feeling a little down, too?"

"Yeah. I really am. It's so strange to think of this whole thing coming to an end and all of us going our separate ways."

We began to reminisce, and I could see that Bobby wanted to talk his feelings out a little bit. Though I knew my family would be wondering what had become of me, I hung around and listened.

Meanwhile, upstairs, Mom and Dad arrived back in our rooms and began to get worried as my absence lengthened. Pretty quickly they started out to look for me.

I guess I had been out of the room a little less than half an hour when I spotted Daddy striding firmly toward us from the elevators. I saw that look on his face which said I was in trouble. I thought to myself, *This could mean a scene. Bobby's going to end up feeling worse than before. He'll think he's responsible for getting me into trouble with Daddy.* My whole plan of offering him comfort was suddenly backfiring.

I quickly decided what to do.

"Where have you been?" Daddy demanded as he walked up.

"Oh, just standing here talking with Bobby a few minutes. I came down to get a snack out of one of the machines." Keeping cool and smiling, I was trying to keep a lid on the situation and spare Bobby. That turned out not to be such a wise decision.

"You've been gone over thirty minutes. Didn't it occur to you we might get worried about you this time of night?" My attempt to be cool had been seen as total indifference.

I persisted with my plan. "Well, no, I didn't think it was any big deal. We were just having a harmless conversation."

"No big deal?" Daddy glared.

"Why, what's wrong? Did you need me for something?" Now I was beginning to feel very uncomfortable and angry, too.

"You just come upstairs with me right now."

I had set down a full ice bucket and candy bar on a chair across the hall, and I turned to pick them up.

"I said now!" Daddy was furious.

"I'm just getting the ice bucket," I explained, still hoping my cool attitude would control the situation and make it work out as I wanted. Instead, Daddy strode back to the elevators with me, leaving Bobby behind, feeling exactly as I had not wanted him to feel.

Daddy continued, "You act as if you can just come and go as you please—like you couldn't care less what worry it might cause anybody else."

I wanted to say I was sorry, but I couldn't. I was locked into my routine of being cool, despite its obvious failure. I felt trapped by my own behavior. And Daddy was getting madder by the minute.

The whole family was gathered in my room. "I found her chatting in the hall off the lobby with Bobby," Daddy announced. "She doesn't seem to understand why we might have been worried."

I flushed with anger and embarrassment.

Daddy turned back to me. "Now just what was so important for the two of you to be talking about so intently at this hour?"

"Well, we were both feeling a little sad about tonight. Especially Bobby."

"What do *you* two have to be so sad about?" Daddy's tone was more demanding than inquiring.

Resenting his condescending attitude, I snapped back, "If you don't know, I'm not going to tell you!"

Nothing I could have said would have enraged my dad more at that moment.

"What did you say?" he yelled.

The ice bucket fell from my hand and sent ice sailing across the floor.

Daddy grabbed my arm. "Don't you ever talk to me that way!" I began to pull away as he tried to lay me over his knee for a spanking. In the struggle, Daddy's arm slipped and his elbow struck me in the head.

"Oh, my God!" I screamed. "You hit me in the head!" I proceeded to fall over on the bed, crying. That distracted him for a moment and picked up sympathy for me from my sisters. In fact, the whole scene must have looked pretty bad, and a couple of the girls had started crying. My mom had even yelled out, "Pat, be careful!" during the struggle.

The phone rang. My dad answered it and after a minute said, "Look, Bobby, I know you think it's your fault, but it's not. This is entirely between Debby and me. I'm sorry, but I can't talk right now. Goodbye."

Daddy turned to me, glaring. I felt my forehead. A nice lump was rising, just the evidence I needed to make my dad out to be the villain and me the victim.

The phone rang again. Daddy turned to pick it up. I looked over at Laury. She was lying on the bed, seething with anger at my father for being so rough with me. She looked back at me as if to say, "Don't you hate him for this?"

It was just the response I had wanted. But at that very moment, something clicked in my mind. The whole scene flashed before me—and, strangely, I could see it from my dad's point of view as well as my own. I had never been quite so free to do that before. The anger drained away, and I couldn't savor the expression on Laury's face any longer. I smiled to indicate that everything was going to be all right.

I turned and walked into the bathroom and began to wash my face. Bobby had called Daddy back, and this time my father couldn't get off the line so quickly. As the cool water rinsed my face, I looked in the mirror—and laughed. I was an amusing picture, with big red eyes and that throbbing lump on my forehead. The whole thing had been pretty silly, actually.

Then I saw Daddy's face in the mirror. He wasn't glaring. He put a hand on my shoulder and said, "Debby, why don't you meet me in my room in a minute?"

I dried my face and left the bathroom. Laury was still smoldering. My smile drew a bewildered stare from her.

I peeked into my parents' room. Daddy was sitting on the bed alone. Hearing my footsteps, he turned and smiled. "Come and sit beside me, honey." As I did, he put his arm around me and looked into my face. "I'm really sorry I gave you that crack on the head. I didn't mean to."

"I know you didn't. It's not as bad as it looks," I smiled. "You know how sensitive my skin is."

"Well, I overreacted down in the lobby, but it just seemed like you couldn't have cared less that we were all so worried."

"Yeah, I know. I was just trying to keep things calm in front of Bobby, but I'm really sorry I upset you."

Daddy hugged me. I wrapped my arms around him and squeezed tight, too. "You know, Deb, we've come a long way to be able to talk like this. It really feels good."

"It sure does."

A few minutes later I went back to my room. I could see Laury was still having trouble with her anger, so I sat down on her bed and stroked her hair.

"Don't be angry with him, Laury. I'm not."

"He had no right to hit you in the head like that!"

"It was just an accident; besides, I really bugged him by the way I was acting."

Silence.

"In fact, we both really apologized to each other in there. He told me he was sorry he hit me and that he hadn't meant to do it."

"Really?"

"Yeah. Besides, all of us are a little emotional tonight. C'mon, Lor, you can see I'm not feeling bad about what happened. Just forget about it."

She smiled and we hugged for a moment, too. The night had become special. For Daddy and me to resolve a conflict in that way was a miracle, and an even greater miracle was to find myself talking to Laury the way I did. It made me think of that night in Tokyo when Cherry had helped me give up my anger.

YWAM

"Do you expect me to stay in Bible school all my life?"

"Debby, that's not what we have in mind." My father's voice was steady and sympathetic, but it was the same story all over again. He was telling me no. Once again the battle was over my ever-increasing desire to start my own career by going into a studio and doing some recording on my own.

"Honey"—it was my mother speaking—"you've spent a good year at the Vineyard School. It's given you some real strength in your walk with the Lord. Please give some more time to laying that foundation. If you cut a single by yourself and achieve almost any measure of popularity because of it, the pressures on you will be really tough. We know. We've walked through it. You really need to wait."

I moaned.

"Debby," Daddy continued, "not only will you be getting more grounded in the Word, but you'll also be adding some practical experience to the training you got in Bible school. That's why I think the opportunity to go to Youth With A Mission is such a good one. You really ought to think about it.

"The Lord's timing is the really important thing. To move ahead or drag behind His schedule is dangerous. And you're in danger of getting ahead, of moving too fast."

"That's easy for you to say, but I feel like I'm going no-where. I wish I saw some end to all this up ahead."

"We really know how you feel, honey," my mother said. "We've faced the same frustrations. I wish you could believe us when we tell you there's wisdom in waiting. God is not wasting your time, even though it feels that way sometimes."

That conversation went on a long time. I was sure I'd never be fully convinced of what they were saying.

How did they know if I was ready or not to begin my own career? Maybe God's timing was now, and they were just being overprotective. Their opinions were not necessarily in-fallible, and if I listened to their advice, I could be making a big mistake!

I was frustrated by the whole situation, but this time, in-stead of obstinately choosing my will over my parents', I took the decision to the Lord. In my year at the Vineyard School, I had come to value those quiet times with the Lord. More and more, I was learning to hear His voice.

As I spent time in prayer one morning, I remembered the conversation I had had with Kenn Gulliksen about trusting God to lead me through my parents. I started to get a clear picture of which approach to take to be able to make the right choice for my future. Relieved of any pressure, I went in to tell my mother what I had decided.

"Mom, I've prayed about what I should be doing this fall, and I think the Lord has shown me."

Mother looked back at me apprehensively. She was prob-ably half expecting that I had just made up my mind and was using the Lord's name to back me up.

"Okay, what do you think you're supposed to do?"

"Well, since you and Daddy are feeling uncomfortable about my pursuing a singing career, I can see the Lord might be showing me it's too soon."

I could feel my mother relax as I continued.

"You both seem to feel pretty good about my spending three-and-a-half months with Youth With A Mission, and maybe that's the Lord, too. I've decided to trust God to show me exactly what He wants me to do through you and Daddy. All I ask is that you pray and ask the Lord to show you. Just make sure you don't base your decision on your feelings, but on what you believe He says to you. Then if you decide I should go, I'll trust God to bless me and prepare me for whatever comes next."

Mom smiled and hugged me. "I'm really proud of you," she said, "and Daddy and I will pray about it and let you know as soon as we come to a decision."

A day or two later we were having breakfast, and Mom and Dad told me they had indeed prayed.

"We do feel it's what the Lord wants, honey," Daddy said.

"And besides, it's only for three-and-a-half months," Mom chimed in.

"Okay, that's good enough for me. I'll call this afternoon and set it up. Besides, it'll give me something to do while Gabri's gone. He leaves tomorrow for Israel, and then goes on to Europe where his dad is working on a movie." Although Gabri and I were not "dating," we still saw each other constantly and struggled with being "good friends."

The next week Mom and Laury and I drove over to the YWAM (pronounced "why-wham") complex in nearby Sunland. The center consisted of two little houses behind a parking lot. An auditorium which also served as a dining area was a few blocks away. The houses were used for dorms and office space. There was another house elsewhere for single male students. After a brief tour, Laury and I filled out enrollment forms for the discipleship training program, and Mom wrote the check for our tuition.

Classes commenced a week later. At orientation, I learned that YWAM was founded in the sixties by a man named Loren Cunningham. Its purpose is to train young Christians in discipleship and equip them to take the gospel to others, especially those in foreign lands.

YWAM was a new and disturbing environment, far from the comfort to which I was accustomed. Besides the daily classes and intense studying, I had the job of taking care of the guest quarters. That involved changing linens, scrubbing sinks and bathtubs, cleaning toilets, vacuuming. . . . I was not thrilled with any of these tasks; I didn't even know how to perform some of them. I could imagine cleaning up after a husband, a man I loved, but it wasn't very pleasant playing maid for someone I didn't even know.

That was especially true the day I had to clean a room occupied by a particularly hairy man. Loose curly black hair was all over the bathroom. I was managing all right until I discovered that it is impossible to wipe hair out of a bathtub with a sponge. Hair clung to the sponge just long enough to be transferred to another part of the slick white porcelain. Very frustrated and disgusted, I finally phoned my friend, Donna.

"I'm going to throw up if I don't finish this job soon," I told her.

Laughing, she told me to try wet Kleenex. I thanked her for all her help and went to find some. Amazingly enough, the tip worked. I began to think I could handle any domestic chore.

Some people found it horrifying that I'd never done more than make my own bed and occasionally dust a table. They made comments like, "I feel sorry for the guy who marries you!" But I figured that even though I might iron a hole in a shirt on the first try, when the time came for me to use household appliances or a mop and pail, I'd learn quickly enough.

Hard work and discipline were the keynotes of life at YWAM. Each morning we rose early for a quick breakfast, after which we were to spend an hour in private prayer and Bible study. Then each of us reported to our assigned groups for more prayer and discussion in the company of seven or eight other people.

That first morning I found my way to the small stage in the main auditorium where my group would be meeting. A few minutes before 9:00, several of us converged on the stage. Soon, the whole group had arrived, and we had arranged ourselves in a circle on the floor. The last to join the circle was our leader.

"Good morning. My name's John Towers. We'll be together, a bit like a family, throughout this session of the Discipleship Training School. This meeting is supposed to be a place where we can share our concerns for prayer—and just talk about things as the Lord leads. This morning, we'll take a little time to get acquainted. I'd like each of you in turn to tell us your name and a little about yourself."

There were two guys and five girls—including Laury—in our group. Our ages ranged from eighteen to twenty-five. Some were recent converts whose pasts involved drugs, sex, and Eastern religions. Others were like me, from Christian homes and with nothing much to brag about in terms of outrageous pasts. Consequently, our conversions, if they could be called that, were much less dramatic.

Most of the hour had passed by the time everyone had had a chance to say something. For the last ten minutes, John Towers went on to explain some of the other things we'd be doing in the group.

"One of our most important priorities will be to pray for various nations. We'll emphasize countries where Youth With A Mission is at work. Then, too, as the Holy Spirit leads, we'll intercede for nations that He brings to our attention. We also want to pray about different political issues our country faces. We all really need to be seeking the Lord in prayer for our country. God has promised to heal our land if we, His people, will humble ourselves, and pray, and seek His face, and turn from our wicked ways. It says that in the Bible in 2 Chronicles 7:14."

I left the meeting that morning feeling unsettled. I had just gone through many changes during my year at the Vineyard Bible School. I had recently accepted the responsibility for getting my life together spiritually, and now I was making new commitments with regard to our government, country, and even the other countries of the world. It seemed like more than I was ready to handle.

The next thing on the agenda was the regular morning assembly in the auditorium. We met each day between ten and noon for a time of worship and teaching. The singing was always uplifting and refreshing. The teaching varied according to the different speakers who were asked to lecture. Usually one speaker would be with us for about a week. He or she would teach in the morning session and then again, usually, in the evening session. A woman named Reona Peterson stands out in my memory. She is a missionary who actually went into Albania, one of the countries most sealed off from the gospel in the whole world. I had read her book, *Tomorrow You Die,* with total absorption.

"We're all experts at praying for God's blessing," she said as she addressed us one evening. "But we want His blessings only for the sake of the blessing. That's wrong. We must set ourselves to think *why* God should bless us. Look at the sixty-seventh Psalm: 'May God be gracious to us and bless us,' it says, 'and make his face to shine upon us.'

"But why should He do this? We find the answer to that in the next verse: 'That thy way may be known upon earth, thy saving power among all nations.' There, that's it! God wants to prosper you, but true prosperity is having such a fullness of resources that you are able to supply the needs of *others*— their spiritual, emotional, and physical needs alike. That is God's best for you. God, through you, for others. The reason God blesses us is to extend His kingdom around the world. And that's why we're here. To learn to spread the gospel to every creature. Anything less than that is insufficient.

"Listen to me! Good is always the enemy of the best. God has a perfect will regarding everything in our lives. Anything other than that perfect will is an enemy.

"Stop and think of the implications of that for your life. Several choices are available to you in terms of how you want to spend your life, or even the next six months. You may have a choice between going to school or getting a job. Or you may have a choice between shopping for shoes or visiting a friend. There's nothing wrong with any of those things.

None of them is like robbing a bank or committing adultery. But if you get a job when it was God's will for you to go to school, then it would be a sin for you to get a job. Good things are the enemy of the best thing. And the best thing is God's perfect will for you and me—moment by moment.

"You know, we Christians are all used to singing these pretty songs about how we love the Lord and give up everything to follow Him, but most of us don't even think about what we are saying. For example, how many times have you sung the words, 'Father, I adore you. Lay my life before You,' when there have been some areas in your lives that you have not completely turned over to Him.

"So, you ask, how can I know if I'm in God's perfect will? One of the most important things we can do to discover that is to carefully and objectively examine our motives for what we're doing or wanting to do. For example, why did you come to this discipleship training school? Because a friend was coming, and you wanted to be with him or her? Because your parents sent you? Because you wanted to be the best Christian in your neighborhood? Because you wanted to get away from some situation or person? Or was it because God told you to come here? . . .

". . . Ask the Lord to show you what He's trying to do in your life while you're here. Tell Him you want to live in His perfect will. And that to do that, you're willing to lay aside anything—even the good things. You need to get your priorities straight and not let anything stand between you and the perfect will of God."

That night after Reona's session, I drove back to the housing area and went straight to my room to try to digest everything I had heard. My whole concept of what life as a Christian should be was being shaken—in fact, completely uprooted. I had been living with the comfortable idea that, as a Christian, all I had to do was give up some things and let the Lord make some changes in me. Then I could live out my life with as few problems as possible. He would help me to be successful in what I chose to do, eventually provide a husband

and a family for me, and finally, I would die a peaceful death and live happily ever after in heaven.

From my first day at YWAM, that storybook life was challenged, but never so intensely as this night with Reona's teaching ringing in my ears. I was trying to sort it all out, when my roommate Kathy walked in, looking as dazed as I felt.

"Hi. You sure made it back here quickly," she said, as she dropped her books on the little twin bed beside mine.

"Yeah, I didn't feel much like socializing tonight. Too much to think about."

"I know what you mean. Reona affected me pretty strongly, too."

Kathy was my age and had been raised in a Christian home and gone to church all of her life; our backgrounds were very similar. I knew she must be feeling a lot of the same things I was, and I was glad we could talk.

"She's an incredible lady. I don't think I've ever met anyone so committed to the Lord and the things He's called her to do," I said.

"Yeah. The more she talked, the lower I sank in my chair, thinking how hard it is for me to discipline myself just to get up early in the morning."

"I know," I said. "I couldn't help but think how this afternoon I was patting myself on the back after finishing my chores—commending myself for my deep spiritual dedication. Somehow I wasn't quite so proud of myself when I listened to Reona."

"I guess we shouldn't be so hard on ourselves," Kathy commented. "I mean, maybe we do have a long way to go, but we've already grown a lot, too."

"You're probably right. Still, I'm completely confused and frustrated. I think that 'good-being-the-enemy-of-the-best' stuff is what got to me the most. I have a hard enough time figuring out good versus bad, without having to figure out 'best versus good.' Does that make any sense?"

"Well, maybe we're both crazy, but it sure does to me."

We got ready for bed and turned out the lights. I'm not sure if Kathy went right off to sleep or not, but I certainly didn't. Thoughts rambled through my brain for hours. What kind of future was ahead for me? How much of it would be governed by the choices I made? On one hand, a simple life with few challenges and responsibilities seemed pretty appealing. On the other hand, an exciting life like Reona's sounded intriguing: miracles, the hand of God working so clearly, people's lives being wonderfully changed.

There was another side to it, too. Reona had gone into Albania to distribute Bibles and Christian literature. That was when the miracles had happened. But there had also been a price to pay. She had made sacrifices, spent literally hours praying each day—and combined her praying with lengthy fasts. It was unimaginable. Or was it? Could I pay the price? I didn't know.

Meanwhile, there was lots to do. With classes and meetings every morning and most evenings during the week, we had afternoons free to take care of our chores and handle other practical matters. We also went out in teams to engage in various kinds of evangelistic outreach on some Wednesday evenings or Saturdays.

YWAM maintained a coffee house on Van Nuys Boulevard in the heart of the San Fernando Valley. The boulevard was regularly jammed on Wednesday evenings with young people, mostly teenagers, cruising its lanes in their cars and pickups. Our purpose was to draw some of them into the coffee house and there expose them to the gospel.

On the night my team was scheduled to work at the coffee house, a Christian drama group was to put on a production based on Calvin Miller's book *The Singer,* which tells the story of Jesus in a poetic allegory. My group leader, John Towers, was the leader this particular night.

"Okay, gang, let's gather around for prayer," he directed after most of us had arrived. It was 6:00. The boulevard would be crowded in another hour. "Dear Lord," John began, "we're here to serve You, to bring glory to Your name. Cleanse our hearts and minds, and direct us by Your Spirit to speak with wisdom and boldness to those who come here tonight. We ask Your special grace and help for those who are putting on *The Singer*. We ask You to draw the people off the street and into this room whose hearts will be open to receive from You. In Jesus' name, amen."

John looked around the circle. "We need two or three pairs of you to fan out into the streets to pass out leaflets about the coffee house. Who'll volunteer?"

I wanted to hide, but I was shamed into volunteering when Laury stepped forward eagerly. John handed over the leaflets and sent us out the door. I looked at Laury when we got out on the sidewalk, hesitating.

"What's the matter, Deb?"

"I hate this kind of thing—walking up to complete strangers. . . ."

"It's not so bad," she chuckled. "C'mon, walk along with me a few minutes. Then you can try it."

I accompanied her up the street and watched as she gleefully pressed the flyers into the hands of all kinds of unsuspecting people. Most of them didn't seem to resent it. Rather, they seemed to warm up to Laury's friendly manner. I marvelled.

At the end of the block she turned to me. "Ready to try it yourself?"

I blanched, saying nothing as she gave me several leaflets.

"Just hand them out to everyone you pass by."

I nodded dumbly as I turned and looked up the street. In a moment, the "walk" sign lit up, and I compelled myself to start walking. I looked frantically for some sweet little old lady to hand a leaflet to. Not one appeared. Instead, the sidewalk was rapidly filling with assorted teenagers. Bearing down on us were two guys who were undoubtedly linemen on some high school football team. They were looking right at us, so I didn't have to catch their eyes.

"Hi," I blurted. "Wanna come to our coffee house tonight?" I stuck out my hand with two leaflets pinched between my thumb and forefinger.

They stopped, looked at each other, shrugged, and took the papers, without saying a word.

"It's free," I added as they walked away, but they just kept moving.

Next came three young girls. They looked to be about twelve or thirteen—not quite so intimidating.

"Hi. Here's something to tell you about our coffee house. Coffee and donuts are free, and it's just down the street. At 9:00 there's going to be a play, too."

"What's the play?" one of the girls asked.

"Well, it's a play called *The Singer,* and it's sort of a parable with a deeper meaning," I explained rather weakly.

"Oh, you mean it's religious or something?" one of the other girls asked.

"Sort of, but not really. I mean it's not like being in church or anything. I really think you'll like it."

I saw one of the girls roll her eyes, as if to say to the others that she would not even think of going.

Completely discouraged, I said, "Well, hope I'll see you there," and walked away, immediately thinking of several other things I wished I had said.

I didn't like walking up to complete strangers on the street. I didn't like people accosting me in public places. Why should I do it to others?

Still—those girls—I felt I knew where they were coming from. I'd been there only a few years ago. I really wanted to help them.

Going out on the streets was a good way to reach them. I'd heard lots of people tell how they met Christ through street evangelists. But was that the most effective way for me?

Something was happening. I wouldn't be happy—I couldn't be happy—unless I knew I was serving God, that I was helping people like those girls to meet God and to experience His love. But I knew that I had to do it in a way that was right for me.

The next afternoon I got a letter from Gabri.

Dear Debby,

I'm in Austria now. This is the fourth letter I've written you and still no answer. What's going on? What can I do to get a letter from you?

Aha! I have an idea. To alleviate any symptoms of writer's cramp, I will enclose a "multiple choice" letter. You need only take a few moments to check the desired response and then post it back to me (I've even included a stamp).

Everyone here is fine. The movie's going well. Vienna is lovely and I miss you a lot.

Love,
Gabri

I smiled as I read over my multiple choices. For instance, I could check off one of the following as reasons why I hadn't written: (a) I'm too busy; (b) I have a new boyfriend; (c) I can't find a pen; (d) none of the above.

I opened the drawer and put the letter in with the other three. With all the rethinking my time at YWAM was forcing me to do, I sometimes felt utterly paralyzed. Was this God's best—or was it only good? What did God think about my relationship with Gabri? I'd gotten that clear leading back in Bible school to let the relationship go. Now what? Should I write him back or let go entirely? My priorities were changing. I was seeking God's *best*, and I wanted to serve Him first of all. How did Gabri fit in? Did he fit in at all? I had no answers.

Meanwhile, my season with YWAM was drawing to a close. Almost all the group I'd enrolled with were scheduled for a missionary trip into Mexico. Laury and I, however, had plans to go to Scandinavia on a singing tour with our parents.

Laury had wanted to go to Mexico with the group from YWAM, but I was more pleased by the prospect of our trip.

My questions about Gabri were unanswered. He arrived home from his trip to Israel and Europe shortly before we were scheduled to leave for Scandinavia. My mother, Gabri's sister Monsita, her boyfriend Terry, and I drove down to the airport to meet him.

I still felt so unsure about our relationship. That's why I'd asked Mom to go with us. I figured if she came along it wouldn't seem like Gabri and I were that serious about each other.

We all waited in the international arrivals area. Finally he made it through customs and came out to meet us. We walked up to each other. He eyed me warily as he put his arm around my shoulders.

"Hi," he said, without actually looking at me.

"Hi." I wrapped one arm around his waist.

He greeted Monsita with a kiss and Terry with a hug. Before I knew it, Monsita and I were tagging along behind, while Gabri and my mother headed across the lobby together. He obviously had been hurt by my lack of communication, and his defenses were up.

We saw each other that night, and I tried to explain why I hadn't written—how Reona Peterson had influenced me, the burden I felt to reach out to others. Talking was hard, because I wasn't sure I understood my feelings myself. Gradually, during the next two weeks before I left for Scandinavia, the ice thawed a bit, but still I wondered where we stood.

On a chilly Tuesday afternoon my family and I took off from Los Angeles International Airport for Oslo. We were scheduled for what proved to be an exhausting tour of Norway, Sweden, Finland, Denmark, and Holland. But we did not sing in the usual round of theaters and nightclubs. It was organized as a Christian tour, and we appeared in auditoriums and churches.

As the tour went on, it occurred to me that God was giving me a chance to test out some of my new priorities. The other kids got to try their wings by ministering in Mexico. I got to try mine in Scandinavia. And it was, as I said, exhausting. Often we had to travel all night and half the next day to arrive in time for our next appearance. The accommodations got pretty rustic sometimes. It was as rough as anything I could remember.

But we were singing for the Lord. Everything we did was to point the people in our audiences to Him. Sometimes we had opportunities to invite them to come forward after the program to acknowledge Christ openly and be counseled. Watching various ones respond—some of them were teen-aged girls—really felt good. I was getting a taste of what ministering in public was like. My new priorities seemed to be getting some validation.

When I got back from the tour, I called Donna. Excited that I was home, she promised to come right over. I was eager to see her, too.

Donna and I had lived across the street from each other from the time we were small children. We went to the West-lake School for Girls together for several years, and then drifted in and out of each other's lives as we grew up. After graduating from high school we became closer than we had ever been.

Now we are the best of friends. We have shared so many experiences with each other, both good and bad, that to this day we can spend literally hours reminiscing about them. I think a few of those memories are worth sharing.

One day, when we were about twelve years old, Donna, another good friend of ours, and I went to "our tree," a huge fir in front of one of the bungalows of the Beverly Hills Hotel, which was less than a block away from all three of our homes. We referred to it as "ours" because it was under this tree that we would regularly sit and share stolen cigarettes. We were all certain that we looked older than our ages, and we felt very mature smoking out in the open like that, instead of crouching down in the bushes behind any one of our houses.

On this particular day, however, our smoking plans were aborted. We discovered two little white dogs that seemed to be lost. We put them in my yard and, playing detective, set out to find their owner. Around the corner from the Beverly Hills Hotel we saw a panicky man searching through the bushes. Dressed in a chauffeur's outfit, he became our first clue.

Casually walking up to him, we asked, "What are you looking for?"

He was so preoccupied he didn't even answer us.

"It couldn't be little white dogs, could it?" I asked with a knowing smile.

He looked up. "Have you found them?"

"Yes, and we'll get them for you," I promised.

First relief and then a smile spread across the man's face.

"You have no idea how happy this is going to make their owner . . . Elizabeth Taylor," he said.

Wow! I thought. *We've stumbled onto a gold mine. Reward* was ringing loud in my mind. With dreams of buying out the candy shop in the hotel, we ran to my house and grabbed the dogs. We ran even faster on the way back.

Our dreams of being candy-rich were shattered when we only got a token amount to split among us, but several days later we received sweet, handwritten notes from Miss Taylor. (I think I still have mine.)

I remember another time that the three of us were together, this time staying overnight at Donna's home. We turned out the lights in the bedroom at 9:00 and set the alarm to awaken us at midnight. We were sure everyone in the house would be asleep by then, and we could safely sneak some cigarettes. Around midnight, we lit up, giggling at each other, trying to blow smoke rings and choking on the inhaled smoke. Soon we heard footsteps coming down the hall. We could tell it was Donna's mother. In sheer panic, we threw the cigarettes to different corners of the room. One ended up under a pile of clothes, another in a rubber wastebasket, while the third one went out the window to smolder among some plants.

When Donna's mom opened the door, we were all tucked

in, pretending to be asleep. Unfortunately, the swirling smoke from all corners of the room gave us away.

"What have your girls been doing?" Mrs. Freberg demanded.

"Nothing," we echoed from far beneath the covers, pretending to be roused from the deepest of sleep.

A brief investigation proved us liars, and we got a much-deserved lecture for having stupidly created a fire hazard by our attempts to conceal the evidence. I was grateful not to have been in my own home that night. If I had been, I would have received a good spanking in addition to the lecture.

Other escapades were just as embarrassing, if not quite so dangerous. One day, during our early teens, infatuated with a couple of boys on the same block but worried they might think we were still too young and flat-chested, Donna and I padded our bras before calling on them. We stuffed them with the nearest thing handy—toilet paper, way too much toilet paper. We then strutted across the street, sure that the brand new "us" would be irresistible, even to thirteen-year-old boys who had little interest yet in girls, flat-chested or not. When the boys' mother answered the door to tell us they weren't home, she looked us over with an amused smile. Donna and I looked at each other, embarrassed. Realizing that she had seen through our guise, we quickly asked to use her bathroom. Moments later, we came out, smiling and flat-chested again, thanked her and rushed away, leaving a badly clogged, overflowing toilet behind.

Looking back, it seems that whenever Donna and I got together, what started out to be a conventional experience turned into an adventure. Since Donna had grown up under more lenient circumstances than I had, she knew about a lot of things I'd never been exposed to. I regarded her as a link to a world I knew little about. Later, after Donna met the Lord, our friendship took on a deeper dimension.

Donna, once the steady girlfriend of Gabri's older brother, Miguel, was close to the Ferrer family, especially Gabri. Though she cautioned me about rushing into anything too serious, Donna thought Gabri was the best thing that could happen to me. There had been little jealousy when I began to spend time with him, instead of with her. That was important to me. I backed away from relationships when overly possessive friends, especially girls, demanded more attention than I felt I could give.

Donna was one of the few people I really trusted. We talked freely and as often as we could. That's why I called her first thing after returning from the tour. I knew she could be counted on to listen *and* to respond honestly and without hesitation to anything I would say.

"How was Scandinavia?" she asked me when we went out for a drive that afternoon.

"Okay, I guess."

"What's the matter?"

"I had another one of those career talks with my parents while we were on tour."

"You mean about letting you go out on your own?"

"Yeah."

"And they still say no?"

"That's right. And I got another free lecture on patience and God's timing. I'm sick of this. I feel like I'm wasting so much time. Am I going to have a career? What's happening with my relationship with Gabri? I still have all these questions with no answers."

"How are things between you two these days?"

"A little better. He was pretty hurt when I didn't write while I was at YWAM. But we had a couple of good talks after he got back from Europe. I wrote him some from Scandinavia, and he called to welcome me home."

We pulled into Donna's driveway and continued talking for hours. That pastime was something we did quite often. Those long talks were good for me. Donna was someone my age who really understood me. And, ever since she had become a Christian, she could look at my problems more objectively than I could and would often encourage me to trust the Lord to work them out.

You Light Up My Life

"Debby, is that you?" It was my mother's voice, and she sounded excited about something. I had been out all day, but I can't really remember what I had been doing. It must not have been too important, though. None of my days had been too colorful since I had gotten back from Scandinavia, and I was becoming very frustrated.

"Yeah. I'm in the kitchen," I answered.

My mother came sailing into the room, all smiles.

"Honey, Mike Curb brought over a cassette of a great song today, and he wants you to think about recording it."

"You're kidding." I was a bit puzzled at my mother's positive attitude about the whole thing.

"No, I'm not kidding," she laughed. "Daddy's in the den. He'll play it for you. It's called 'You Light Up My Life.' "

What I heard was a relatively old-fashioned ballad—nice, but nothing new. As I listened, I thought about all the resistance I had gotten from my parents every time Mike had suggested I record on my own. I was beginning to think it would never happen. Now this.

"Well, what do you think?" my dad said as he clicked off the recorder.

"It's really nice—I guess I'm just stunned. I thought maybe you didn't ever want me to record on my own." I half expected my mom to say, "Oh, we didn't mean for you to sing

83

it alone. We thought you and the girls could do it in four-part harmony!"

Instead, she explained that all they ever wanted was for me to wait for God's timing.

"We think we know you pretty well. And we've noticed great changes in you. You're strong and stable enough now to handle whatever comes from all this. And we think this song would be the perfect place for you to start."

I could see they knew how hard it had been for me to wait so long, and somehow feeling their support and encouragement made me know that the timing was right. The waiting hadn't been for nothing.

"Well, how about it? Do you want to give it a try?" my dad asked, smiling.

"What do you think!" I laughed.

It was during that same conversation that the three of us discussed the song's lyrics. How perfectly they described our relationship with the Lord. Obviously, it was written as a love song—the theme for a movie by the same name that was to be released that summer (1977). Still, it was perfect. What better way to launch a career than to have your first recording be a song which could be interpreted as a song of love and praise to the Lord. Everything was falling into place.

A few days later I was in a small studio with Michael Lloyd, the man who had produced the last few records my sisters and I had made. Michael helped me make my first demo record of the song. The tape was rushed off to New York, where Joe Brooks, the creator of both the song and the movie, would listen and decide if he wanted me to come to New York and record the song for public release.

The girl who had recorded the song for the film had had a run-in with Joe, and now he was looking for someone to record the song for the single radio version. Mike Curb had found out about the whole thing while viewing a special screening of the movie. He had suggested my name to Joe.

I was pleasantly surprised when Mike received word from

New York that Joe liked the demo and wanted me to fly in to record with him as soon as possible.

My mother and I had made tentative plans to go to Ohio to visit some very close friends for her birthday in late April. It would work out perfectly for us to fly to New York for the recording session and then go to Ohio afterwards.

It seemed strange that after traveling in and out of the country for nine years with my family I should get so excited boarding another plane for New York. Not that I thought this record was going to catapult me to the heights of stardom or anything. I was simply elated to have a chance to travel across the country, to work with a record producer, and to sing a beautiful song—all by myself. As it turned out, I was very glad my mother had gone with me to share in my excitement and to help ease the tension I would later encounter.

We arrived at Kennedy Airport in the evening, went to our hotel, got settled in our rooms, had dinner, and called it a night. The next morning, we were picked up by Joe's secretary and driven to his office, where I was to get acquainted with Joe and run through the song before going to the studio.

Joe's office was very impressive. The walls were lined with Clio awards (television commercials' answer to the Grammys). I had not known that Joe was probably one of the most successful commercial jingle writers around. *You Light Up My Life* was his first movie (he wrote and produced it). We had a very nice first meeting, and everything seemed to be going as smoothly as the demo had gone.

"Well, shall we get down to business and run through the song a couple of times before we go over to the studio?" Joe asked.

"Sure." I was a little worried that without all of the benefits of recording studio sound, Joe might not be so impressed with me.

He began to play on a Rhodes electric piano, and I began to sing. I didn't get past the first verse before he stopped me and made some suggestions as to how I should phrase a couple of lines. We started over, and I tried my best to accommodate him. This time, we got a little farther, but somewhere in the chorus he stopped again and made some more corrections. A little embarrassed, I tried to explain that Mike Curb had asked me to sing it the way I was singing it.

"I don't care what Mike said. I want it this way," he said very abruptly.

The tension began. I understood that this song was very close to him, and I knew he had a lot riding on the record. But I was the singer. Didn't I have anything valid to contribute?

By the time we left for the studio, I was upset and felt very insecure. I was very glad my mother, though she had been silent, was there for moral support. The studio was much larger than the one I had recorded the demo in, and all the musicians were there, ready and waiting for us to begin our work.

I walked out into the studio, and my mother, the engineer, and Joe went in the control room. It was great to hear the movie soundtrack with the full orchestra and forty strings, and I began to sing with all I had in me. Joe abruptly cut me off in the middle of a note.

"No, that's not right! Remember what I told you in my office?"

"Okay. I'll try it again."

I was very frustrated. I was trying to make my version sound a little different from the one by the other singer. We were different artists, with different interpretations, and I didn't want to make a replica of the cassette I had heard at home. But every time I tried to vary the melody in the least, Joe cut me off and made me do it again. The friction was building between Joe and me, and we didn't seem to be getting anywhere. I asked Joe to excuse me for a moment, and I went straight to the restroom to try to calm down. My mother followed me.

"What's wrong?" she asked.

"He's making me crazy! Every time I want to do something

that's right for me, he cuts me off and makes me feel like an idiot!"

"Why don't we just pray and ask the Lord to be here with us and take control of the whole session."

My mother took my hands and, there in New York, in the restroom of a recording studio, we committed the song and the recording into His hands, asking Him to relieve all the tension and to replace it with His peace.

I felt much better. I realized I only had to concentrate on the lyrics and sing from my heart to the Lord, and He would work out the rest.

Things ran smoothly after that. When I closed my eyes and sang, it was as if I were really alone with God. Whenever I opened my eyes, I could see my mother with her hands cupped over her mouth. I knew she was praying.

In a few more takes, Joe and I were happy, even though I had added a few things to the song. I thanked Joe for giving me such an opportunity, and he thanked me for coming out to sing his song. The pressure was off, and we parted friends.

The next morning, we were off to Ohio to see our friends. It struck me as strange that my mom, who had certainly been anything but a "stage mother" type, could not stop talking about the new record.

"I'm telling you, Deb, I just have the greatest feeling about this song. I know it's going to be a hit!"

I wanted to forget about it. That way, if it hit, I would be pleasantly surprised, and if it didn't, I wouldn't be embarrassed.

Singer/songwriter Paul Williams and his wife also happened to be on the plane, sitting directly behind us. "Deb, you should tell Paul about your new record!" my mother whispered to me excitedly. I had met him before, but I really didn't see why he should care one way or the other. "He doesn't want to hear about it," I replied in a low voice. "Let's just skip it."

Undaunted, my mother took out a tape recorder and began

to play a cassette of the song. I pretended to be looking out the window, fascinated by a particular cloud formation. When she held the lead sheet up slightly over her head and started humming the words, I knew she had left subtlety behind. Needless to say, Paul didn't fly over the back of my chair to meet me. My mother finally had to introduce herself in the Cleveland airport to tell him about me and my new song. Paul was very nice, but he didn't ask for my autograph or anything. Two years later, it was my pleasure to appear with Paul at the Sahara Hotel in Lake Tahoe, and we laughed together remembering the whole scene.

During our stay in Ohio, our friends took us to John Davidson's nightclub act. Backstage after the show, my mother proceeded to give John the exciting news about my budding career and suggested he might want to have me on one night while he was guest-hosting the *Tonight* show. He, too, was very gracious about it all, and I have since done the *Tonight* show with him on a couple of different occasions.

Though embarrassed, I couldn't help wondering if there wasn't something to my mother's exuberance. After all, for two years she had been anything but excited about my pursuing a show business career. Now there was no stopping her. I would just have to wait and see.

On the last leg of the trip home, I had some time to reflect on my conversation with Kenn Gulliksen. He had been right about waiting on God to reveal His will through my parents; I couldn't deny that. But sometimes the uncertainty of it all had seemed unbearable. Now I was faced with a different sort of uncertainty, and I began to see the wisdom of Kenn's advice. Timing would be all-important in the coming months. Maybe waiting wasn't the worst thing in the world after all.

May and June passed uneventfully with the exception of a few concerts here and there with the family. That summer, though, we spent more concentrated time on the road. The scenario was much as usual, except Cherry had gotten married, moved away with her husband, and was no longer performing. The first inkling I had that something unusual was happening with my record came late in the summer, when I was at the Holiday House in Pittsburgh. Towards the end of our engagement there, my dad suggested I start to sing "You Light Up My Life" in the show. He felt I would probably need the experience if and when the song was a hit and people started expecting to hear it.

Somewhat excited and extremely nervous, I performed solo for the very first time. Lindy introduced me; then she and Laury stepped back by the orchestra and I moved to center stage alone. I don't know if people were surprised that an established singer's daughter could actually sing well, or that such a loud, belting voice could come from a small-framed, five-foot-four blonde, but their response seemed to imply that my performance had exceeded their expectations. Their response certainly exceeded mine.

Things couldn't have gone better for the first time, I thought as I walked back to the dressing room.

Later, a D.J. from a local radio station came backstage to meet the family. He informed us that my record was beginning to get airplay across the country and had appeared on the Gavin Sheet that week.

The Gavin Sheet is a weekly report published by an ex-disc jockey named Bill Gavin. Radio stations across the country report to Gavin any new songs in their programs that are getting good response. Anyone in the record business trying to keep up with the industry's up-and-coming hit singles subscribes to this report.

I couldn't believe my ears. It was almost as if he were talking about someone else. My mother was beaming.

"I knew it, Deb. And this is just the beginning!"

I was thrilled; yet at the same time I couldn't help wondering if maybe that's all this was—a beginning.

After all, lots of records get this far without really going on to be big hits, I reasoned. That thought didn't bring me down, though. Even if it was just a beginning, it was exciting enough. I figured I was lucky to have gotten that far.

A couple of weeks later, we returned to L.A. to perform at

Magic Mountain again. I was now singing "You Light Up My Life" in every show, and the audience seemed to respond more and more. During that engagement, we got word that the record had hit the charts with a "bullet." A bullet is a mark printed next to the song title that signifies that the song will be found in a higher position on the charts the following week. When a song "loses its bullet," it's a sign that the song has reached its peak.

Mike Curb and all the promotion men from our record label were excited about the record's potential. While we were still at Magic Mountain, a man named Jerry Weintraub came to see the show. He is well known as a manager of entertainers like Frank Sinatra, Neil Diamond, John Denver, and others. He came because he wanted to negotiate a contract with my father to do a TV series. After seeing our show, he was convinced he could arrange something with one of the three networks for my father, possibly even for the whole family. He also approached our two managers about my going to Australia with John Denver to be on his TV special.

I couldn't believe that anyone would want me on their TV show! My record was doing very well, but nobody knew who I was. It didn't make sense! Little did I know then that by the time the special aired, "You Light Up My Life" would have been number one on the charts for ten straight weeks, and people would, indeed, know just who I was.

Before I left for Australia, I went on every major talk show in America to promote the record. This sudden rise to fame was all happening so fast, my head was spinning. I could hardly sleep at night, especially as my first appearance on the *Tonight* show approached. I had been nervous doing shows like *Dinah* and *Merv Griffin*, but there is something awesome to every entertainer about the *Tonight* show. I was encouraged knowing that my father was going to come on the show with me, and I knew he would help put me more at ease. My nervousness was still getting the best of me, though, causing headaches and stomachaches. I would daydream about forgetting words, missing notes, or fainting. I almost had myself convinced I just couldn't get through it.

Of course, I did get through it. The Lord was faithful to supply my needs. I was very calm on the show and have been every time I've done the show since.

In early December, I left with my manager, Don Henley, for Australia. It was my first trip apart from my family, and my first adventure as an entertainer touring solo. Australia was absolutely gorgeous, and performing with John Denver was a great experience for me. It was like a paid vacation.

After Christmas that year I was caught up in a whirlwind of press interviews, TV shows, promotional trips, and autograph parties. I had to put together an album to go with the single and a show to take on the road. People were coming out of the woodwork, asking me to do all kinds of things.

Like a dream, the success of "You Light Up My Life" was often unbelievable. My rendition sold over four million copies and stayed in the number one position longer than any other record of the past twenty years. The awards were overwhelming. They were sometimes frightening, too. Because of the song's acclaim, I was asked to sing it at most of the award presentations.

The 1978 Grammy Awards were televised in February. Because the show was live, there was a run-through the day before. My stomach knotted and my head spun as I walked into the rehearsal. John Denver was doing his number. That was kind of reassuring, since I knew him fairly well now. Aside from John, the musicians, and the production crew, the theater was deserted. I began to calm down. But then I went onstage and glanced out at the auditorium.

Looking bigger than life, the stars of the recording industry filled the best seats in the house. Barbra Streisand, Linda Ronstadt, Olivia Newton-John, and many others seemed to be staring at me.

The faces weren't real. They were only enlarged photographs that had been set up while I was getting ready backstage. The crew was using the pictures to facilitate camera blocking. They intended to shoot the expressions of the award contenders and other celebrities during the actual show. My picture was among them. But that didn't make much difference. My mouth was dry and my throat felt tight. When Nelson Riddle's orchestra began to play "You Light Up My Life," the awesome reality of my situation hit me. Debby Boone, who had done so much less than the other stars, was going to have to stand up in front of them and sing.

I struggled through rehearsal, trying not to think about the next night. Later, I couldn't eat or sleep. All the time I kept telling myself, "I don't believe this is going to happen."

It wasn't any easier the next day. So many people had said "You Light Up My Life" was the pick for Record of the Year that I began to believe it myself. I didn't know what I'd say if "You Light Up My Life" did win, and I was still afraid my singing was going to be a disaster. Gabri was scared, too. His hands were clammier than mine. He was so nervous that several people commented later, "Whenever the camera panned in on you two, Gabri was chewing his gum like a madman."

Before the show began, there were last-minute walk-throughs in evening clothes and makeup. I had to be ready early and then wait a long time for my turn to come. In my dressing room, I tried everything to calm down. I prayed. I sat still. I paced. And then flowers arrived from a girlfriend. The card had a Scripture verse on it: "My grace is sufficient for you, for my power is made perfect in weakness" (2 Corinthians 12:9).

I read the card many times to absorb the calming message. Soon it was time to take my place in the audience with Gabri. I felt a surge of panic when Paul Williams and Linda Ronstadt took their seats across the aisle from us. Knowing I'd have to get up and sing for them in a few minutes nearly caused me to forget about winning anything. Even after the award presentations began, I worried about singing instead. Record of the Year came near the end of the ceremonies, after it was my turn to sing. Since winning wasn't my immediate concern, the announcement that I'd won Best New Artist came very unexpectedly. I was caught entirely off-guard.

Trying not to shuffle down the aisle with a blank look on my face, I strode onto the stage confidently and said: "Well, I certainly didn't expect *this* one."

What a jerk! That was all but telling the audience that what I really expected was the big award at the end—Record of the Year. I could have kicked myself fifty times as I walked back to my seat.

When my turn to sing finally came, I was amazed at how quickly my body calmed down. The shaking and stomach-aches stopped as I walked out on the stage. My mind collected almost as fast. At first, my eyes kept focusing on the stars in the audience, switching from one well-known face to another as they looked back at me. But as the house lights dimmed, the audience faded from view and I relaxed into my song.

Then I thought, *This is it. The moment you've been panicking about for weeks is here.* As suddenly as I'd become composed, I began to fall apart again. My eyes focused in the dark and I could see everyone watching me. I wondered what they were thinking. Finally I realized that my mind wasn't where it was supposed to be. The minute I started singing to God, "You give me hope to carry on," I felt a surge of confidence. The Lord *was* coming through, being my strength when I was at my weakest point.

This experience cemented a valuable lesson I had been learning since that first appearance on the *Tonight* show. I would have to hold onto that knowledge closely for the next few months, and I'm sure for my entire career. I realized, through much prayer for God's peace and strength, that I could not get through this show, or any highly pressured situation, successfully unless I took my eyes off everything and everyone except the Lord. I could not allow myself to contemplate what people would think of me, or if I was as talented as other performers, or anything except "Christ in me, the hope of glory." God had been directing my career from the start, and He alone would keep it going.

"You Light Up My Life" received two other awards, but it didn't win Record of the Year. The auditorium was hushed, and when "Hotel California" by the Eagles was named, I tried not to look disappointed. For ten or fifteen minutes I felt badly defeated. At last I began to comfort myself as I thought about my award as Best New Artist. If I'd won Record of the Year instead, it might have meant people thought that "You Light Up My Life" was a one-shot deal and Debby Boone a one-hit artist, never to be heard from again. Votes for Best New Artist meant people were confident my success would continue. I was pleased and grateful.

Tahoe

Gabri and I continued to keep our relationship in a kind of limbo throughout 1977. In some ways we were closer than ever. We saw each other often. I always wanted him with me to share in all the excitement of my new career, and I needed him with me as I began to feel the pressures. Many times I felt inadequate to meet the demands made on me professionally, but Gabri was always around to support and encourage me. We tried to keep the focus off the romantic potential that existed between us. Because of this, there often seemed to be an underlying tension present. Each time it surfaced and exploded, we tried to give up the relationship entirely. That was worse. Patiently, we kept on with our strange and undefined arrangement, something that would have been harder to do if life had not become such a swirl of activity with the success of "You Light Up My Life."

Overnight, I had become a celebrity. It seemed like everyone in the world was asking to hear me sing my song. When I wasn't onstage singing, I was asked to give advice, support causes, or sell something. My fan mail was so heavy I wasn't sure I'd ever be able to answer it all. When I was on the road, churches vied for my attendance at their services. Businesses wanted to involve me in everything from Debby Boone dolls to wristwatches with my face on the dial instead of Mickey

Mouse's. My private moments were limited to hotel rooms and the occasional days when I could rest at home.

At times, I was tempted to move out of my parents' house. I certainly could afford my own apartment, even a house. People would remark, "You're twenty-one and making enough money to support yourself. Why are you still living at home?" I thought about moving just to shut them up, but there were good reasons to live at home. The most important was that my family had a way of bringing me back down to earth. I was never allowed to think of myself as an almighty star—God's gift to show business. I was still asked to do some grocery shopping, and I still had to give back clothes I had borrowed from my sisters. I even retained my job of cleaning the cat box.

"Is that you, Debby?" Mom called as I shut the back door.

"Yeah, just got home."

"Good. Would you see if you could find time to clean out the cat box now?"

"Listen, I've really had a rough day. That doesn't have to be done right away."

"Look, Debby, it's been three days since the last time you got around to doing it. That has to be done every day, or else the whole family has to put up with the smell because you didn't do your job! If you're too busy to take care of your cat, then maybe you should find another home for it."

I rolled my eyes in frustration and went to clean the cat box, feeling very put upon.

As I look back, I can see my family did me a great service by consistently refusing to be overawed by my instant rise to stardom. Having to clean the cat box every day while my first single was riding the number one position on the charts kept me from taking myself too seriously. It was a healthy balance at a time when a lot of people kept telling me how wonderful and talented I was.

Just as my family helped me, so did Gabri. Ever since things had begun to happen for me career-wise, Gabri had grown increasingly concerned about me. The burden of suc-

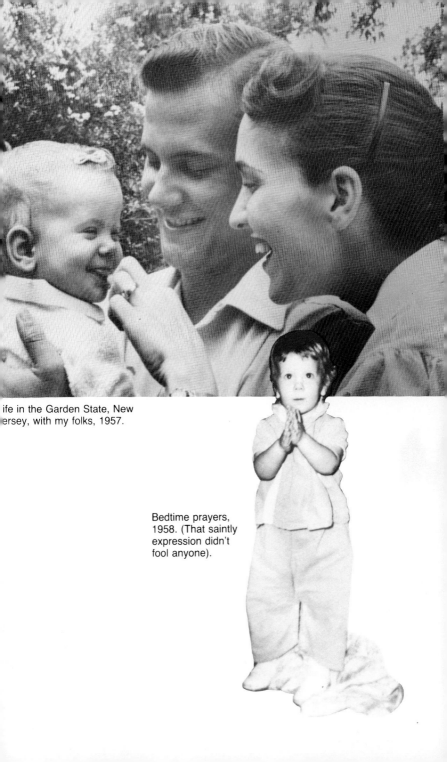

ife in the Garden State, New
ersey, with my folks, 1957.

Bedtime prayers,
1958. (That saintly
expression didn't
fool anyone).

My first television appearance, 1960; I was hooked!

"The Boone Girls" on our first singing tour in Japan—the time of the cigarette incident.

YOUNG AMERICA'S FAVORITE MAGAZINE   SEPTEMBER 1974   75 CENTS

seventeen

THE
NOSTALGIA
BOOM

FIFTY NEW
CLOTHES
FROM
THE 40s
    50s
    60s

"WHY HOLLYWOOD'S
STUCK IN THE
GOOD OLD DAYS"

exercise bugs you
DANCE AWAY YOUR FLAB

BACK TO SCHOOL?
PACK A SKILLET

IN LOVE
FOREVER?

YOUNG AMERICA TODAY:
Growing Up in a Broken Home

WAYS TO
CONTROL YOUR ANGER

HOW A KISS MADE
ME QUIT SMOKING

FLYING SOLO
the world pilot, age 17

Pat Boone
and his daughter
Debby, 17

Photo by Patrick DeMarchelier
Reprinted from SEVENTEEN Magazine
Copyright © 1974 by Tringle Communications, Inc.
All rights reserved

Food fight!

Signing albums in an L.A. record store the day that Gabri visited me.

My unofficial godfather, Perry Como.

Acting debut in "The Gift of the Magi."

A normal day in Hollywood. From left to right: Debbie Reynolds, Debby Boone, Bob Hope, Daddy, Sammy Davis, Jr.

Singing "For me and my gal" with Gene Kelly.

Opening night in Las Vegas with Mr. and Mrs. Kenny Rogers and Mike Curb.

At the Inaugural Gala with President Reagan, Bob Hope, Charlie Pride, and First Lady Nancy.

The wedding, September 1, 1979.

From left to right: Miguel Ferrer, Jose Ferrer, Rosemary Clooney, Gabri, myself, my folks, Donna Freberg, brother Donavan, and flower girl Hannah Cutrona.

Donna Freberg and I at my wedding reception in one of our more solemn moments.

Worshipping at a teaching seminar.

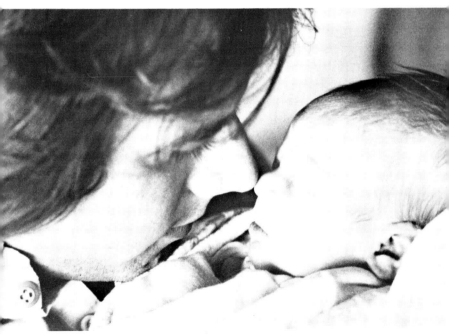

Gabri and Jordan's first father-son talk—he's three days old.

cess, he knew, was too much for me to carry alone. He stayed near at hand, and he prayed for me often.

One night about a month after the Grammys, Gabri was sitting alone in his room, thinking and praying about me. He told the Lord, "I don't see how Debby and I can go on like this much longer. She's not getting the help she needs. Too many of her emotional and spiritual needs aren't being met."

Strangely, as he prayed, Gabri sensed the yellow light of caution change to green. The Lord was saying, "You're right, Gabri. You two can't stay like this much longer. Now is the time to move ahead in your relationship with Debby."

Gabri was stunned. Had he heard right?

He smiled to himself, thinking, *Why is believing God has spoken so much harder when He says something you want to hear, than when He says something you don't want to hear?*

But Gabri was convinced that God had spoken—softly, but distinctly.

When Gabri talked to me, I was filled with mixed emotions. Wasn't this just what I had been waiting for? Could God really be giving us the go-ahead to pursue our relationship on a romantic level? I told Gabri that I was going to have to pray about it on my own and see if I felt that kind of freedom. Oddly enough, after all this time, I was very unsure about my own feelings towards Gabri. I was afraid of commitment, and the state of limbo that we had been experiencing in our relationship felt very comfortable to me—despite the frustrations. The relationship required no real effort or change on my part, and I liked that.

Three months later, I had to go up to Lake Tahoe to appear with my father at the High Sierra Theater in the Sahara Tahoe Hotel. I was having fun working with him. Our relationship was growing happier all the time. I still marvelled at it—as I'm sure he did, too. Now we shared a great rapport, both on and offstage.

Gabri was a different matter. On the day I was scheduled to leave for Tahoe, he had driven me home from a visit to my nutritionist. I had received word earlier in the day that an interview I'd given to a free-lance journalist months before was finally going to be published in a major magazine. Normally, I wouldn't have worried about it; however, this particular article was intended to deepen the public's perspective of me. The interview had been conducted six months earlier by a good friend, and I had been too open and candid about my personal life.

At the time of the interview, I was frustrated that my relationship with Gabri seemed stale and unfruitful. I didn't know if it was worth salvaging. Not thinking very sensibly or sensitively, I made the statement that I didn't believe I was in love with my boyfriend anymore. I realized immediately how wrong I was to blurt such a private matter out for national publication. The worst part was that I had never told Gabri how I felt at the time.

Now, just when our relationship was starting to go somewhere, an article saying I didn't love him was due to appear. I knew I was in trouble, but I had to tell Gabri about it before he read it for himself. I spelled out the details as we drove home.

The entire incident hit him hard. I couldn't make any excuses, because there were none. I was wrong, and I'd hurt him badly. I knew saying, "I'm sorry," wouldn't help. After driving the last ten miles in silence, Gabri let me out of the car and said coldly, "I'll talk to you later."

I prayed for him and for us the next few days. He had been so sure he had heard the Lord correctly about our getting back together. My mistake was a pitcher of ice water in the face. I knew he was struggling. Should he hang onto what he thought he had heard God say, or should he interpret the article and my unwillingness to make a firm commitment as rejection? I could only pray; I had to catch a plane later that morning. It was really in God's hands.

I didn't hear from Gabri for several days after I arrived in Tahoe. Finally, the phone rang in my dressing room between shows.

"Hello?"

"Debby, we've got to talk about our relationship and get something settled."

"Okay." My heart was pounding.

"I'm coming up there tomorrow. Can I see you in the early afternoon?"

"Yes."

"All right. I'll see you then."

He was usually not that terse. I was intimidated, but I felt kind of good, too. Gabri was calling the shots now. I had to wait and see what the outcome was going to be.

The next day, I awaited Gabri's arrival in the guesthouse where we were staying. I gazed out the window overlooking the lake, reflecting on all that had taken place in the last year and anticipating what the future might hold for Gabri and me.

My thoughts were interrupted by the doorbell. I opened the door, and there was Gabri, his expression cool, his brown eyes watching me from behind amber-colored glasses. Unsure we'd be alone in the house, he suggested a walk.

"Sure." I was barefoot and wearing a T-shirt over rumpled jeans, but I didn't bother changing. Tugging on my tennis shoes, I followed him.

The path down to the lake meandered through pine trees that were tall enough to shade us from all but the most penetrating rays of sun. We walked slowly, side by side, without talking. The area was so quiet I could hear the pine needles bending beneath our feet.

Finally, the trees thinned out and we began scrambling over the huge boulders that replaced them. Gabri asked, "How's the show going?"

"Great."

We found a flat rock near the water and sat down. I gazed out across the lake instead of looking at Gabri. I knew our conversation, once it started, would involve more than just making up. If we did get things straightened out, it would be time to make decisions about the future. This was sort of a win or lose situation, and I seemed to be uncomfortable with either prospect. To lose would mean Gabri was fed up with trying to make things work out for us, and our talk would signal the end. He would walk right out of my life. I certainly didn't want that. To win would mean he was willing to try again—but only with the guarantee of a real commitment on my part. The prospect scared me. I was so afraid of making a mistake.

Gabri was quiet for quite a while. I found myself intrigued. Always before, I was the one who called the shots. I also did most of the talking. Gabri rarely offered an opinion, unless I requested one. Now I wasn't sure if he was going to tell me to forget it or that there was still a chance for us. I realized he was assuming the lead in our relationship. I liked that.

Gabri finally began talking about our problem. I could see that, for the moment, he wasn't feeling much love for me. He reached down for a handful of pebbles and started skipping them across the water.

"I seriously considered heading for New York instead of coming here," he said. "I could move in with my father and enroll at Columbia University."

"Would you really do that?" My voice was softer than usual. I wasn't sure that he still wouldn't fly east.

"Uh-huh. I had to make a decision whether or not I wanted to cope with the problems of being involved with an entertainer."

Gabri knew firsthand about the tremendous strains of such relationships. His parents, Jose Ferrer and Rosemary Clooney, had encountered them all and, sadly, had lost their marriage.

"Lack of privacy, limited time together, separations during tours. . . ." He tossed more pebbles into the water.

I knew what was coming next. I met many attractive and talented men in my business. Many seemed interested in me. There were times when it would have been easy to begin a close relationship with someone else.

"They're serious problems," Gabri said. "The easy thing

would be to go out and find a nice, comfortable girl who would be totally devoted to me," he said. "Someone who would absorb herself in everything I did. Someone with a normal life and a normal schedule."

He paused for a second.

"The worst part of it is that for the last four months since we decided we could move ahead in our relationship, I've never felt any real commitment from you. It has always been half-hearted, with lots of provisions for getting out easily. Yet, you expect all of the fulfilling benefits that go along with a true commitment. It just doesn't work that way."

"But, Gabri, I'm afraid. I don't want to hurt you if things can't work out."

He looked at me.

"I'm willing to take that chance."

We both began tossing stones into the lake.

"Debby, are you really worried about hurting me, or do you not want to feel responsible or guilty if things don't work out? There is a difference."

Those words cut to the quick, but Gabri had not said them in anger. He was right. My motives had been very self-centered. I hadn't been protecting Gabri; I had been protecting myself. I was leaving lots of room, in case I grew tired of the relationship or met someone else whom I was attracted to. As long as no commitments were made, no one could blame me.

I learned a lot about myself that afternoon. Being able to take an honest look at my faults was half the battle. I respected Gabri for loving me enough to point them out and to help me deal with them. In the end we both agreed our relationship was worth giving all we possibly could to make it work.

Walking slowly back to the house, we began to talk about our nearly aborted trip to Hawaii and Japan. Combining a vacation with my appearance at the Tokyo Music Festival, the trip was to be our first alone. Naturally, this required the approval of my parents, a big step for them. My older sister, Lindy, and her husband, Doug, could not believe that Mom and Dad were allowing us to go.

"Boy, have things changed since we were dating!" they said.

I needed an escort to the Tokyo Music Festival, and I couldn't think of anyone I would rather have come with me than Gabri. Initially, wondering what my parents would say, I hesitated suggesting him. Later, sensing the time was right, I approached them confidently, saying that I really thought Gabri was the one to come with me.

As it turned out, I needn't have worried about my parents' response. They'd been praying about who should accompany me to Japan and had decided already that Gabri was a good choice.

"You've proven that your relationship with Gabri is under God's control," my mother said. She liked Gabri, especially for his serious commitment to the Lord and the way in which he encouraged me in my faith.

Daddy also agreed, but I could tell he found the situation hard to believe. His head was nodding, but his eyes asked, "Am I really letting my daughter and her boyfriend go away to Hawaii for five days and then to Japan for another week?"

In the past, my parents always worried about my choice of friends, feeling that I picked some who weren't spiritually uplifting to me, friends who held me back instead of helping me. Gabri was one of the few people in my life whom they thought could be a completely beneficial influence.

June 1, 1978, was my father's forty-fourth birthday. We were all in the lakeside house at Tahoe. Two close friends of my parents and their wives came to the house to help us celebrate. One of those couples was Albie Pearson and his wife, the pastor whose word had meant so much during my struggle with Kevin. Late in the afternoon, we took time out to pray together. Soon after we began praying, Daddy was called out of the room for a phone call. While he was gone,

Albie took my hand in one of his and Gabri's hand in the other.

"Do you love this guy?" he asked me.

"Yes."

"Do you love her?" he asked Gabri.

"Sure."

He smiled at us and said, "I can see the Lord likes this relationship. But let it develop naturally. Don't try to force anything."

As I heard those words, I felt warm all over. I knew it was an indication from the Lord that Gabri and I were heading in the right direction. Big tears began rolling down my cheeks.

My mother and I were both crying when Daddy came back into the room.

"What did I just miss?" he asked.

"These two are supposed to be together," Albie said, putting his arms around Gabri and me.

A panicky look crossed my father's face. "You mean forever?"

"Yes."

As we were leaving to go out to dinner, I grabbed Gabri by the arm and pulled him away from the others into a side room.

"Can you believe it?" I said, hugging him. "After three years of ups and downs, it finally looks like we've made it."

Hawaii/Tokyo

Not long after I returned from Lake Tahoe, Gabri and I had to leave for Hawaii. I still could hardly believe my parents had said it would be all right for him to accompany me on the trip. Sure, we would have separate rooms and all that, but their permission still reflected a lot of trust. The development was especially strange to me, because I had accused them for several years of not trusting me. Only in recent months had I grown more willing to accept their restrictions without loud protest.

Los Angeles International Airport was very busy the day Gabri and I left on our trip. We checked our bags and moved to the boarding area without any extra attention. That is, with one exception. Two photographers snapped pictures of us as we were coming up an escalator. One of their pictures later appeared with a *National Enquirer* article which proclaimed loudly that Debby Boone and her boyfriend were "frolicking in Hawaii."

The truth was less sensational but more important. Gabri and I had just gone through a rough time—a crisis of sorts—in Tahoe. But that in itself, together with Albie Pearson's counsel, had helped us achieve a new degree of commitment to each other. Now we were going to take this trip together. I wondered what it would mean in terms of our future.

We changed planes in Honolulu and flew on to the big island of Hawaii, where my brother-in-law, Dan O'Neill, met us at the Kona airport. Dan and Cherry were both employed at the YWAM center there, one of many branches located all over the world. They were all part of the same organization I had been involved with for three months in Sunland, California. Laury was also working in the program.

After Gabri checked us in at the Kona Hilton, we drove over to YWAM. I hadn't seen Cherry and Laury for months and was eager to catch up on their lives. Dan took Gabri on a tour of the YWAM base, and the three of us sat down on the couch in Cherry and Dan's small living room and we all began talking at once.

Cherry, who'd been married to Dan since October 1975, loved living in Hawaii and working with YWAM. She was teaching young children at a YWAM-sponsored school. The staff there was developing new principles in primary education; introducing a structured lifestyle at an early age so that the children would feel greater security and stability. Immediately relating this to my work at Hathaway and my inherent love for kids, I was fascinated with the progress Cherry described.

"Knowing exactly what their teachers expect, even if strict discipline is involved, seems to make the kids a lot happier," Cherry said.

Laury was in charge of hospitality at YWAM. The job included responsibility for keeping the guest rooms clean. Laughing to myself, I wondered if she had learned the wet Kleenex trick yet.

When my sisters asked how Gabri and I were getting along, I smiled and told them what Albie Pearson had said in Lake Tahoe.

Cherry and Laury were aware of the unusual relationship Gabri and I had had for the last three years, and loving him as they did, they were ecstatic to hear the news.

"This time I think we're going to be together for good," I said.

"I'm sure it's all going to work out great," Cherry said, smiling confidently.

Seeing Cherry so happy, looking strong and vibrant, feeling useful, excited about her work and her marriage, was wonderful. The last time I'd seen Cherry, she had looked emaciated and miserable. For almost ten years she had suffered from *anorexia nervosa,* a syndrome that manifests itself in uncontrollable weight loss. It usually begins with habitual dieting and is totally consuming—sometimes fatal. Victims often look worse than concentration camp inmates.

No one knew exactly when or how Cherry became a victim of anorexia. Perhaps it started during her preteens when she stayed up half the night doing homework. Always a perfectionist, imposing the highest standards on herself, Cherry wanted every grade to be an "A." Still insulated with a layer of baby fat, she began taking Mom's diet pills at thirteen, when she started worrying about her figure. She learned to like the way the pills made her feel. She could whip out a great term paper after taking them.

As soon as Mother realized that her diet pills were disappearing, she flushed the remaining supply down the toilet. In response Cherry, who looked old enough to be a Mrs. Boone, picked up prescription refills at the drugstore. By the time Mom discovered what was happening and cancelled the prescription, it was too late. Strangely addicted to dieting, and having no appetite, Cherry lost weight even without the pills. Within eight months, Cherry dropped from about a hundred and forty to less than ninety pounds. Out of control, the disorder worsened during the next five years.

At first, the family thought Cherry's problem was behavioral. Sometimes we all got fed up because we thought she could stop starving herself if she wanted to. We figured she wasn't trying.

"Why do you keep doing this to yourself?" we asked.

Cherry couldn't explain. Doctors were unable to help. Prayer seemed ineffective.

Finally, Cherry saw that the root of her problem was buried in an inability to accept herself as she was. She needed to develop a healthy self-image. After a few years of drawing on her future husband's spiritual strength and self-discipline, the situation began to improve. She finally began to put on some weight when she started seeing a Christian psychologist about the problem. Living in Hawaii had proved to be really helpful, too. She was learning to fight off the disorder, and all of us were grateful for the breakthrough.

As do most sisters who get together after a long separation, we reminisced about less serious times growing up. Laury was quick to remind me that I usually had been the instigator of trouble and the ringleader whenever my sisters and I were disobedient. Yet often, if we were caught, they were punished instead of me.

When Laury and I were about six and seven, we shared a bedroom. Every afternoon about 1:00 my mother sent us to our room for a nap. One day we were horsing around instead of sleeping and accidentally knocked over a big lamp. The clatter was sure to attract attention. I heard someone coming down the hall toward our room. Jumping under the covers, I left Laury to face our angry father. He caught her out of bed and she got the spanking, while I pretended to wake up startled from all the noise.

Spankings, especially from my father, were not just a perfunctory pat on the behind. He meant for us to remember them and used a slipper, belt, or anything else that stung. The number of whacks on our bare bottoms depended as much on our reaction to being caught as the offense itself. We could expect more if we had lied or talked back.

Often with tears still fresh in our eyes, the four of us would go up to my room and compare war wounds. Bending over, we'd back up to the mirror to see whose backsides had the reddest marks. Mine were always the worst, mainly because I had the most sensitive skin.

Another time that Laury was paddled when I deserved it came when we were playing "truth or dare." The game involved a choice between answering any embarrassing questions the other players could think up or accepting a dare to do crazy or sometimes dangerous things. One summer at camp, I made others eat horse manure and even tried it myself. At home, I had been known to dare my sisters to jump from tall trees or rooftops.

This time I made Laury take off her clothes and ride her bicycle around the driveway. She was only nine, nothing too obscene, but there she went after we had taunted her sufficiently. Our family home is right on a busy intersection, and Laury had to ride around our circular driveway and out onto the sidewalk—five times in all. Lindy and I hid in the bushes, laughing hysterically, especially when a tour bus drove by to show out-of-state visitors "the homes of the stars."

Laury was tooling around on her fourth trip, when our mother came back from a shopping trip. The car screeched to a halt in the driveway, and Laury was grabbed off that bike almost quicker than we knew it. Lindy and I stifled our laughter as we watched Laury's bare behind disappear through the front door under my mother's strong right arm.

I never said a word to protect Laury. She had once told me she'd rather take the punishment than watch me get paddled. That was fine with me. I figured at the time that if she was that dumb, I wouldn't stand in her way. Today I recognize that Laury wasn't dumb. What I mistook as stupidity was really the seed of warm sensitivity and compassion for other people.

From early on in my life I had a mean streak, and at times I could be a very proficient liar. People always believed me, because I looked so innocent. Most of the time I was very kind to people outside the family, so if I did make up a story, I could pull it off easily.

I remember an incident from my childhood when my schemes worked perfectly. A little boy named Peter, a third-grade classmate of mine, was a studious and obedient child, whom the teacher just loved. But Peter was never strong or devious enough to protect himself from me. One day in art class, frightened because I was chasing him, he overturned a chair in my path. It clamped my finger against a desk, causing a painful blood blister. Vengefully, I told the teacher that

Peter had thrown the chair without reason. The talking-to he received didn't seem like sufficient punishment for hurting me. Sometime later, as we were standing silently in line waiting to use the drinking fountain, I turned around and hollered at him, "How dare you call me that, Peter!" Working up tears, I continued shouting that he'd sworn at me. I told the teacher that I could never repeat the words that Peter said. They were just too awful.

"But I could write them down," I suggested helpfully. I racked my brain for every cuss word I had ever heard. Putting on my most angelic expression, I handed a long list to the teacher and watched her scan the paper.

"He called you *all* of these?"

"Yes, ma'am," I answered, shedding another tear for good measure.

As Peter moved his short legs rapidly to keep up with the teacher, who was marching him straight toward the principal's office, I smiled.

Lying also helped me draw attention to myself whenever I felt I wasn't getting enough—which was fairly often. For example, I created a terrible scene at a summer camp in the High Sierras. Walking through the woods on the way to dinner, I got the idea to make up a story about a strange man trying to assault me. I covered myself with mud and made scratch marks on my face. Working myself into hysteria, I ran into the camp cafeteria screaming, "There's an awful-looking man with long black hair after me. He chased me into the bushes. I fell down. It was awful. . . ." By that time, I was crying and shaking so hard that I almost believed the fantasy myself. Camp counselors rushed into the woods, looking for the maniac. During the panic, I was the center of attention. I loved it.

Once again, in that small room in Hawaii, I was the center of attention, but at least this time I had come by it honestly.

"Let's forget about the past for a second. I want to know when you and Gabri are going to get married?" Laury rerouted our conversation abruptly.

"I don't know," I said thoughtfully, remembering Albie's admonition not to rush into anything. "I have to get used to the idea first."

As soon as Dan and Gabri returned, Laury whisked me away to meet her new boyfriend, a guy she had become interested in there on the YWAM base. Before it got too late, Gabri and I headed back to the hotel to get some much needed sleep.

Hawaii was a great place for me to unwind after months of touring. The nicest part about it was that Gabri could wake up, walk down the hall, knock on my door, and come in to share the first part of the day with me. Those morning devotionals gave me a sense of fulfillment I'd never experienced before. We'd order up orange juice and a pot of coffee, sit out on our private veranda, and spend an hour looking out at the sky and ocean, praying and praising God.

On the Sunday we were there, we held our own little church service. Laury, Dan and Cherry, and another couple came to sing, pray, and read the Bible with us while the sun shone brightly and the surf crashed in the background.

Gabri and I were learning what it's like to be together constantly. Like my mother, I am a private person. Sometimes, I need to be completely alone. *Am I comfortable enough with Gabri to ask for time to myself?* I wondered. It turned out that he was less possessive than I was. I never thought I'd be, but I was actually disturbed when he excused himself and went to be alone in his room. Always before, my relationship with guys had been imbalanced. They wanted more from me than I ever asked of them. Now it was different.

Another discovery we made was that simply spending time together served to strengthen our relationship. I guess that doesn't sound too revolutionary. I had known several couples, though, married and otherwise, who spent a lot of time apart from one another and claimed that their time together was richer because of it. I had always thought I would choose the "absence makes the heart grow fonder" method for myself, but it just didn't work with Gabri and me. The more time we spent together, the more we really appreciated each other.

I recalled the regulation in the Old Testament that exempted a man from work or military service during the first year of his marriage. The purpose was that he might be free to spend time at home making his bride happy (Deuteronomy 24:5). If that law were enforced today, it might have a radical effect on the divorce rate. The uncluttered time Gabri and I spent in Hawaii was a season when our love and caring for each other grew deeper.

The vacation was also a time when both Gabri and I had to be cautious that, while we were growing emotionally and spiritually, our physical relationship did not follow suit. That was the one area we had agreed would have to stand still temporarily. Some people would say we were only frustrating normal desires. If we had opened up to that aspect of sharing our love, they reason, we would have enjoyed even greater growth.

Both Gabri and I disagree with that kind of thinking. The way we saw it, then and now, if we had given in to our sexual desires before marriage, we would have planted seeds destructive to the life of that marriage. We both would have known that the other, despite any Christian affirmations, was willing to enjoy sex apart from marriage. Such knowledge would have served as grounds for suspicion after marriage.

Even more important than the consequences of giving in to sexual desires are the advantages of refraining. For example, the trust we were building in each other and in ourselves was invaluable. I later experienced a real object lesson concerning this point.

Gabri and I were asked to speak in Del Mar, California, for an Easter service, and our accommodation for Saturday night was a beautiful two-bedroom condominium. The condominium was part of a very exclusive country club. We spent that evening enjoying a marvelous dinner served to us in the living room, in front of a fireplace. When dinner was over, and we were curled up on the couch watching TV, I began to play up to Gabri physically. I began massaging his shoulders and kissing him and telling him how much I loved him, but he seemed to be completely unresponsive to me. I was embarrassed and felt rejected, and I began pouting in a chair across the room.

"What's wrong?" Gabri finally asked.

"Nothing," I lied.

"Come on, you're not sitting in that uncomfortable chair, frowning, because everything's fine. Come over here and let's talk."

Gabri made room for me on the couch, and I got up and went to sit beside him.

"Okay, let's have it," Gabri said, as he pulled me closer to him.

"I just feel like you are ignoring me tonight. I mean, I was being so affectionate a while ago, and you practically acted like I wasn't here."

Gabri hugged me comfortingly. "I'm sorry," he said. "It's just that this setup is a little too perfect tonight, and I don't feel in control. I love you so much, and I don't want to let something happen we would both be sorry for. The only way I can see to prevent it is to not let anything get started at all."

I realized then how blessed I was to have someone like Gabri, who loved me so much that he would be careful always to protect me, even when it meant truly denying himself. It was the exact reverse of the selfish demand, "If you love me, prove it." I had never felt Gabri's love more strongly than that night.

Gabri and I didn't want to sound self-righteous about our moral stands. We understood very well the temptations facing single Christians.

The Lord had shown me that purity or "virginity" was not at all just a physical state but was equally a matter of the mind and emotions. I once took pride in the fact that I had maintained my virginity, when many of my friends had not.

However, I soon began to learn that conversations about sex with friends, dirty jokes I laughed at and repeated, sexually oriented TV shows and movies I had watched were all taking away from my own purity.

After all, we are spirit, soul, and body, and all aspects of our being are affected by the things we subject ourselves to. I got convicted particularly about the magazine articles I read on topics like "sexual hangups" or "How to please your partner," etc. . . . Like most girls, I figured I should prepare myself for experiences ahead. God showed me that, instead of preparing myself, I was filling my mind with preconceived ideas about something that was highly individual, instead of relying on Him to develop naturally a healthy sexual relationship between my husband and me.

As I began curbing these outer influences, I saw something wonderful. I realized that, in the Lord, virginity could be restored—maybe not physically, but emotionally, mentally, and spiritually. We don't have to live under condemnation or the feeling that, "Well, I've already blown it, so what's the use." It is never too late for the Lord to take a situation and turn it around for His glory.

Often when Gabri and I talked about our future, there were flashes of temptation to get married quickly. However, we were learning the advantages of being patient. Timing was indeed important. At the moment, I was not inclined to interrupt my career; and, of course, Gabri was still in college.

"Maybe in two years . . . three years. . . ." My thoughts weren't entirely clear. I'd always loved the idea of having kids when I was really young, to minimize the age difference. The twenty-year age span between my parents and their first child seemed ideal. Yet I didn't love the idea enough to rush into marriage and get tied down before I had a chance to test my independence.

One day, toward the end of our stay on the island of Hawaii, Gabri suggested going to the beach. After making numerous inquiries, he couldn't find one nearby.

"This is absurd," he said. "In Los Angeles, you drive twenty minutes and you're at a beach. Here we are in Hawaii, and the closest beach is forty-five minutes away."

It was Gabri's first time on the Islands. Looking out at the shoreline of hard, black lava flows, I told him that the volcanic landscape was supposed to be one of the special beauties of the Kona coast. I promised there'd be plenty of beaches when we went to Oahu.

We finally found a place to go snorkeling that afternoon. Underwater, the fish along the reefs were fascinating. On the surface, the wind blew froth in our faces, and the waves tossed us back and forth. It was rough, but there was little danger.

We spent an hour too long in the choppy water. When we came out, our skin was puckered, and everything seemed to be bobbing and weaving.

I laughed. We looked like a couple of prunes.

The next day, we flew over to Honolulu, where Gabri and I stayed on Waikiki.

"See," I told him, "there are convenient beaches in the Islands."

"Convenient, but crowded," he observed.

Gabri and I both like French cuisine, so we went to dinner at a Gallic restaurant where my father had taken me several years before.

"I wonder if he ever thought I'd come here again under these circumstances," I said as Gabri sat down across the table from me.

After eating, we wandered across the street to the International Marketplace and window-shopped. Gabri loved to look for unique gifts.

Two years before, on my birthday, he had given me a handcarved, delicately painted bust of an angel that he'd found in Vienna and a gold necklace from Israel with the word "angel" spelled in Hebrew. The following birthday, he had given me a gold pin in the shape of an eighth note. The round part of the note is in the shape of a heart with diamond clips in it. As always, I had that jewelry with me.

"Remember the first birthday present you gave me?" Gabri asked, his eyes twinkling.

"Tennis shoes." That had been almost three years before. "I'll be more imaginative this August," I promised.

We spent the next day cruising around on an outrigger canoe with about eight other people, all strangers. No one recognized me, maybe because they had more important things to do, like bailing water out of the boat. The sea was rough, and the canoe overturned almost immediately. We spent the next two hours struggling to right the craft in the crashing waves, trying not to step on sharp coral reefs or get bashed by the hull. Finally, we gave up and dragged the sinking boat to shore.

"We must do this more often," Gabri said wryly when we got the water out of our ears.

The vacation ended the following day. As we got ready to leave for Japan, Don Henley, who'd flown out to meet us, gave me a detailed review of the schedule for my appearances during the Tokyo Music Festival. Next to the United States, Japan is the second largest record market, and it's wide open for young American singers. My schedule was loaded with TV and press interviews. Whole days were set aside for radio broadcasts. The tour was going to be very busy.

"We won't have much time together," I told Gabri.

"You'll be just as busy when we get back to the States," Don said.

I nodded. My summer tour would cover twenty-five cities in two months. In between shows there'd be more radio and TV work, preparation for the family Christmas special, and my acting debut in the television special, "Gift of the Magi." There was a lot more to do after that. I needed to find new songs to sing. Mike Curb, president of the company I recorded for, and the men who produced my first two albums were always offering me new material. I had to review it all. Some songs, I liked. Others I didn't.

It tore me up when I had to pretend to be serious singing lyrics like, "You and me, hey, we could be, more than wild creatures and fish in the sea." Other lyrics nearly put me to sleep. Experts in the recording business kept urging me on, trying to convince me that my taste did not always conform to what was commercial on the radio. I knew I needed another hit record, but did that justify cutting records that embarrassed me?

My head was full of such thoughts on our flight to Japan. Then I remembered what my mother said when I had had doubts like this before.

"You're not operating like the world operates," she pointed out. "The world says, 'Now, if you don't have another hit, you're not going to be able to sustain your career.' But your career wasn't put together by the world, and it is not going to be sustained by the world. God makes the plans for whatever will happen to you."

My mother's counsel to her children was never based on what the world would advise, but on what the Lord directed. I knew there were times, like the moment, when He wasn't ready to show me the next move. I needed patience.

Feeling better, I dozed off. An hour later, the stewardess announced dinner. Gabri came down from the 747's lounge, where he and Don had been looking at pictures taken at my last photo session.

"I think they're good, but you probably won't like them," Don said, knowing I was very particular about photographs of myself.

"Maybe I'm too self-conscious," I admitted, smiling. I was in a relaxed mood.

During the night, with the cabin lights dimmed, I let the drone of the jet engines lull me back to sleep. I didn't wake up until after breakfast had been served. Later that day, we landed at the huge airport outside Tokyo. Traffic was a problem near the end of a long ride into the city.

"This is as bad as the freeways in Los Angeles," I said.

"You didn't think all our cars were in the United States?"

Tats Nagashima, our Japanese promoter, responded with a grin.

During the week that followed, I was even busier than expected. In addition to singing in the Festival, where I won the gold prize, I made numerous guest appearances on TV, posed for pictures with local teen idols, greeted thousands of fans, and was constantly interviewed for the media. The reporters were not as pushy, their questions not so blatantly sensational, as some American journalists. They knew Gabri was my boyfriend and that we were traveling together. They let it go at that.

Gabri and I had little time together. Oftentimes, when I was rushing to meet schedule deadlines, he found more interesting things to do. He shopped and explored the city with his sketchbook. I missed him and envied his freedom to move about without an entourage.

In spite of the rough schedule in Japan, we fared quite well. As we left for L.A., we all felt very good about the success of our trip.

Don was glad Gabri had come along. So was I. The trip had been trouble-free, and we all were sure the Lord was responsible for that. Looking back, it seemed more clear than ever that Gabri and I were meant to be together.

Prelude to Summertime

Something came up after I returned from Japan that showed me my relationship with my father had come a long way in four short years. After dinner the first night I was home, my father called to me from the den.

"Deb, could you come in here for a minute?"

"Sure. What's up? You know I still haven't unpacked from the trip."

"Sit down a second, Debby. I'd like to fill you in on some things. You know I've just put some money into this Christian radio station in Flagstaff, Arizona. It looks like it could be a really good thing."

"A Christian radio station. Sounds good."

"I thought you might want to invest some of your money also."

"Hmm. I'll have to find out more about it. I'm not sure I can afford it right now."

"Well, I've already invested some of your money for you."

"What?" A surge of anger and resentment started rising inside me. "How could you do that?" I asked in disbelief.

"Well, Jack [my manager] has your power of attorney. While you were in Japan, he signed the papers and our accountant wrote the check."

"I don't mean *how* could you do that. I mean, how could you *do* that?"

"I invested, too. The opportunity wouldn't have been there if I had waited until you got back."

I tried to stay calm. I was determined not to lose my temper.

"It really bothers me that you would make that kind of decision without talking to me first."

"I figured that if you didn't want to be part of it, you could take your money out anytime you wanted to. It was as if you had been away when it was time to pay tuition for a school you might have wanted to go to. I did it for you, knowing that if you changed your mind, you could always withdraw and get a refund. I was just making it possible for you to be part of something that could turn out to be very important."

"I can understand that. But you need to know, too, that I *wouldn't* feel free to ask for my money back anytime I wanted it. What if the radio station caves in two years from now? I couldn't ask for my money back and let you absorb the whole loss. I just couldn't."

"But I thought I was doing you a favor. I wouldn't have done it if I had known it would upset you."

"I know that; I really do. But if you had just called me first, we could have avoided the whole problem."

"Well, from now on, when I see opportunities I think you might be interested in, I'll be sure to check directly with you first."

"Thanks. Sometimes I just get frustrated . . . well, you know, I have this tiny streak of independence."

We both smiled knowingly.

That conversation helped to set some guidelines for us. More importantly, I learned that we *could* talk. Communicating ideas, feelings, and insights to each other without going through hell and back was possible. What a difference!

That breakthrough set the stage, too, for what came next: another conversation, this time with both parents—about Gabri. The three of us were standing around in the kitchen; I was telling them a bit about the trip to Hawaii and how Cherry and Laury were faring.

"I still can't believe we let you travel alone with Gabri like that," my mother said, changing the subject slightly. I was pretty sure she wanted some direct reassurance that things had gone well in that area, too.

"The *National Enquirer* couldn't believe it either," Daddy added, smiling. "I guess you saw the picture they ran of the two of you."

"Only three dozen people sent me copies," I replied. "That reminds me—Gabri would like me to meet him in New York to visit his dad while we're on our three-month tour. We were looking over the schedule, and there's room to do it around his birthday at the beginning of August. What do you think?"

"Well, uh, where would you stay?" Daddy was obviously feeling a little uneasy about my request.

"There's room in his dad's apartment for both of us. Gabri says I could use the guest room, and he could sleep on the couch in the study."

"Hmmm," Daddy said, his eyebrows raised characteristically as he assumed that friendly expression that could mean anything.

I smiled back. "Gabri and I have spent so much of our time together here in L.A. I think it's important to get acquainted with his dad, too."

"I suppose that's true." Daddy was beginning to relax. "I guess we can work it out."

"Great. I'll make arrangements to fly out of Rhode Island down to New York on July 31. Then I'll meet you at that fair in Montana on August 5. I really do appreciate your trust. We won't betray it."

Not long after that, I got together again with Donna Freberg. We still talked freely and as often as we could, running up huge phone bills when I was out of town.

"All right. I want to know all about your trip. The way I figure it, you and Gabri are either a lot closer now or it's all over," Donna kidded as we drove around that afternoon.

"Definitely a lot closer," I said. "It was important for both of us."

"How did people react to your traveling together?" Donna asked.

"Fine. Since we felt good about it and didn't make a big deal, no one else did either," I explained.

"Is he going to keep on traveling with you?"

"I doubt it. My schedule's too frantic. Besides, Gabri has to teach a Bible class, and then get ready to go back to college," I said.

Donna nodded.

"It could be a mistake to take any more trips with Gabri unless, like the last time, we are sure traveling together is the Lord's will," I added.

"You're right. You need His protection," she said. "Sometimes people are so quick to judge."

"All right, Freberg, I'm hungry. Let's go eat."

Donna steered the car toward Aunt Tilly's, our neighborhood health food store.

Pulling up in front of the store, Donna asked, "Were you able to get any decent food while you were away?"

"Not bad. Of course, in Japan most of the food is natural anyway."

"I'm glad," she said. "I'm sure it can really be difficult to eat correctly on the road."

Donna was probably more concerned than anybody about what I ate. Just a few years before, she had come to a point in her life where she never felt well. She was worn out all the time, suffered headaches, developed stomach trouble, and displayed a number of other disturbing symptoms. No one could figure out what was wrong with her. Not long after she accepted the Lord, an excellent nutritionist helped Donna change her eating habits completely. I was impressed with her discipline and amazed at the fast improvement I saw in her.

Now, I agreed with her that God intends for us to take

special care of our bodies. My body had revolted, too. Besides not eating right, I was once addicted to coffee. When I was in Bible school, I drank fifteen or twenty cups a day. I even carried a thermos around with me. The coffee habit caused my hands to shake almost constantly, sometimes so much that I had to use two hands to get the cup to my mouth without spilling it. One big excuse I had for drinking coffee was that doing so curbed my appetite.

I was really sensitive about any sort of weight problem. Being only five feet, four inches tall, I thought a few extra pounds made me look much too heavy, especially when I was being photographed. Television cameras are the worst. They make everyone look overweight. Whenever I was getting ready to do TV, I went on crash diets. Then, as soon as the show was over, I would go on a binge. Under the guidance of that same nutritionist, however, I was learning to control such erratic eating habits.

I was reaping the benefits, too. Without the vast intake of caffeine, my nervous system balanced out. I was now able to function better when I was subjected to pressure. A healthy diet seemed to give me better control of my weight. I also noticed a big improvement in the condition of my hair and skin.

Since my early teens, when I first became conscious of my looks, I had always worried about my complexion. While most of my friends, especially Donna, had soft, clear skin, mine broke out. I thought it was the most sickening thing that could happen to me. I worked hard to improve my skin, and I still use natural skin products every night to help.

I was very insecure about my physical appearance when I was growing up. There were so many things about myself I didn't appreciate—like the freckles all over my arms. Until I was about fifteen, it could be 110 degrees in the shade, and I'd still wear long sleeves. I thought those freckles were the ugliest things ever. Jokes like, "We could play connect-the-dots on your arms," made it worse. Donna consoled me by telling me she'd never even noticed them.

Donna and I were halfway home from Aunt Tilly's when we noticed a carload of guys following us. Whenever we drove around together we seemed to attract curious males. They pulled up next to us at an unavoidable stoplight, and we tried to ignore their stares. Finally, one of the guys rolled down his window and yelled, "Are you Olivia Newton-John or Debby Boone?"

"Who do you think I am?" I yelled back, laughing.

"I'm not sure!" he answered.

"Well, take a guess!" I teased.

We drove on to the next light, and the same car pulled up beside us. "Okay. You're Olivia Newton-John, aren't you?"

"Right!" Donna and I drove off, laughing.

I found it amusing that I wasn't easily recognized. More often than not, people would say, "You look like Debby Boone," but they never quite believed that's who I was.

Usually, at public events where people expected to see me, I was no longer anonymous. During times like that, privacy was hard to come by. I was grateful for the times when I was just another face in the crowd.

Back at my house, I guess I must have gotten quiet. Donna asked what I was thinking so seriously about.

"About what all this success means. I wonder what God has in mind?"

"What do you mean?"

"Well, as a singer I'm supposed to put a show together that will entertain people. But I'm sure God has more than entertainment in mind. Right?"

"Right."

"Okay, so how do I arrange a show that is really good professionally and which also accomplishes God's purposes?"

"I don't know."

"Neither do I. Maybe I'm trying to take too much responsibility on my shoulders. There are a lot less hectic ways to make a living. I could go back to work with kids, or I could grow a garden in the Midwest. Sometimes, when there's too much pressure and I think of being in show business the rest of my life, having to work constantly like my dad does, I'm ready for a slower-paced life."

"I don't blame you. Even without a struggle, there are times when I'm ready to move away from city life," she agreed.

The next morning, I overslept. I threw on some clothes, hit my face with a washcloth, and rushed to a meeting with my managers. Before going back on the road, I wanted to know more about how my business affairs were being handled. Though I trusted Jack Spina and Don Henley completely and was equally confident in my financial advisors, I was beginning to realize that, before I got much older, I needed to know a lot more about the business side of my career.

Many people assume I am already a millionaire. That exaggeration always amazes me. The money to be made from a hit record, unless one is the songwriter, is not all that impressive. Plus, people either forget, or don't know to begin with, how many expenses an entertainer has to bear. In addition to helping support managers, musicians, agents, and publicists, I am usually responsible for my own expenses and the expenses of any people who travel with me on tour. A similar situation exists when I record singles or albums. I pay the production costs, or at least they are deducted from my royalties. Production costs for an album can run extremely high. Even if my work earns a great deal of money, I only get to keep a portion of it.

My personal managers had power of attorney for me. They collected the money I earned and turned it over to my business manager, who wrote the checks to pay my bills. My own financial transactions were limited to using credit cards and trying to maintain my personal checking account. I didn't completely ignore my finances. I knew when I was doing well and when I wasn't, and I always asked if I could afford it before spending large amounts.

As I entered the office, I couldn't help wondering what people think when they read the list of companies lettered on the door. Cooga Mooga, Inc., a name that means nothing in particular except that my father liked the sound when he once heard a disc jockey chanting it, identifies the Boone holding company. Lamb and Lion Records produce Christian records. Rosina Management is Jack Spina and Don Henley, who manage my father and me. Spoone Music publishes songs. The bottom name on the list is Resi, Incorporated—my new company.

Years before, Donna Freberg's precocious little brother and I had fallen into the habit of thinking up various silly names for each other. One day, I was sitting around exchanging titles with him; first, I'd throw one at him, then he'd toss another back at me. All of a sudden he blurted out, "You, you *residue!*" I burst into laughter. This was not a word I expected to come out of a six-year-old's mouth. He never forgot the incident, and eventually the name stuck. To Donavan, I was "Residue," which was shortened to "Resi." No one ever found out where he learned the word or if he even knew what it meant, but when the time came to name the corporation, the choice was obvious.

Beyond the receptionist's desk was the hallway leading to the private offices. The walls were hung with gold and platinum records, all Daddy's except one—"You Light Up My Life." Heading for Jack's office, I wondered how he ever managed to keep track of the hectic Boone careers. This morning his desk was heaped with correspondence, offers for appearances and endorsements, suggestions for new songs, requests for interviews, and clippings of reviews, stories, and gossip columns. A confirmed bachelor, Jack nonetheless had perfected the protective father role after nearly twenty years of overseeing Daddy's career. He understood the double pressure of rushing around the country and singing two shows a night. He also knew that I enjoyed what I was doing.

"Everything is an adventure for you. You're just like your father," Jack often told me.

That morning, Jack seemed pleased when I told him I

wanted to learn more about the business side of my career.

"I'll arrange for you to meet with your business manager right away," he said.

Though Jack and Don were responsible for advising me on matters pertaining to the sources of my income, John Mucci and Associates helped me handle the money after it came in. That was the difference between a personal manager and a business manager. Jack and Don believed that most entertainers need both.

Personal managers also help develop earning potential. As they screen proposals from agents, producers, and other businessmen, they help establish career direction. They help in the technical areas: hiring musicians, arranging for lighting and sound equipment, and anything else connected with appearances. Setting up transportation and hotels is another way they make it easier for an entertainer to concentrate on performing. Business managers, on the other hand, function as accountants, tax experts, and investment counselors.

Previous earnings from TV appearances with my family and songs recorded with my sisters had been held in trust until I came of age. With that money and the income from other recordings, personal appearances, and concerts, there was no question I needed the help of a business manager.

One of the first things I did when I took on John Mucci as my accountant and business manager was to direct him to give ten percent of my income to the church. As far as my family and I are concerned, tithing is one way of showing the Lord that we know everything we have comes from Him. But it goes deeper than that. I remember our pastor, Jack Hayford, teaching the subject from the Bible in no uncertain terms. It is a mark of elementary submission to God, and it opens the way for blessings by releasing God to work on our behalf as Lord of our finances (cf. Malachi 3:10–12).

After scheduling a meeting with John Mucci for me, Jack began reviewing my summer schedule. In two days I was due in Owensboro, Kentucky, to receive the Golden Plate Award that is given to achievers in various fields. Along with me, an astronaut and Steve Cauthen, the jockey, were to be recipients. The day after those ceremonies, I was to meet my father in Morristown, New Jersey, to begin our tour together. The schedule was packed.

The public seemed to want to see me and my father perform together. We were getting offers that paid more for us together than we could earn separately. I asked Jack if he thought the dual appearances would hurt my chances for solo bookings in the future.

He said he wouldn't be involved with the tour if he thought so. I wouldn't be playing just to the young record buyers who were so important in putting songs among the Top 40. But, he said, I shouldn't forget that my father still had a large following, too.

Then Don came in and began telling me about the movie scripts that were being submitted for my consideration.

He handed me four or five to read. "The others were either too far out in left field, or you wouldn't be available to meet production deadlines." So far, no movie scripts had seemed appealing. Instead, I was very interested in doing a TV special based on O. Henry's "The Gift of the Magi." My managers and my family liked the idea, too.

"Yeah, but can I act?" I joked.

We began to talk about other career opportunities, including the area of endorsements. I didn't like the idea of lending my name to an assortment of unrelated products that I seldom, if ever, used. Nor did I want to overcapitalize on my recent success.

One of my biggest struggles so far had been to accept the responsibility of living up to a very strong image that was established from the beginning. The image was "the straight-laced, All-American Girl," or synonymously, "the daughter of Pat Boone." The fact that my family had always been very open about their Christianity added another dimension to my image. At first, I felt pressure to be something I wasn't, until I realized that all I had to do was be myself. After all, I do lead a very straight life, probably what many people still call the

"All-American Girl." And I am a Christian, meaning I choose to live by Christian principles laid out in the Bible. All of this is true, whether I am in the public eye or not. But I knew from the start that I would have to be careful making professional choices, so that people wouldn't think in any way I was being hypocritical.

One problem I always seem to face is the lyrics of the songs I sing. I learned fast that people really listen to words. If I sang anything that anyone felt was contrary to what I stand for, I was sure to receive letters of criticism. This began as early as "You Light Up My Life." In my wildest dreams, I never would have thought anyone could complain about the lyrics of a song I sang in praise to the Lord, but I was wrong. At the end of the song is a line that says, "It can't be wrong, when it feels so right." From the moment the song became popular, I received letters of disappointment and was forced to defend myself in many interviews. That issue still comes up to this day.

The only people I was aware of who ever found the line questionable were Christians. The letters were all written by Christians, and the interviews where I was asked the question, "How can you justify singing that line?" were always for Christian publications or Christian radio programs. The big concern was that I was in some way promoting the popular philosophy, "If it feels good, do it." Christians have always been taught that good feelings don't always lead to right behavior, and I believe this, too. In fact, I have often been misled by my own feelings. As I thought about it, I could understand why some had found the line in the song questionable. On the other hand, I sang this song to the Lord. Isn't it true that, when you accept the Lord, everything about the relationship *feels* more right than anything ever has before? I certainly saw the line that way when I recorded the song.

Even though I understood some Christians' concern, I knew I hadn't done anything wrong. It seemed to me the energy would be better used in praise and thanks to Him for all the lives that were affected positively by the song.

I received letters that were even more difficult to deal with than the criticism. One was from a woman who wrote, "I've tried to kill myself three times. Please, can you give me any good reason to go on?" Assuming she was sincere, I tried to show her that the Lord provided many reasons for living. Answering that kind of letter always drained me. In such cases, I never knew for sure whether my response was instrumental in affecting lives or was ignored.

It was a welcome relief to get mail from people who simply said, "I know you are busy. Please don't feel that you have to write back. I just want you to know I appreciate everything you're trying to do."

Nonetheless, as long as I combined a singing career with work for the Lord, I knew I'd have to deal with criticism and try to help other people with their problems as well.

After I left the office late that afternoon, I went to spend a quiet evening at home with my folks. I had already signed the contract for this book, but I hadn't begun to write. I was having a hard time getting started. I asked the family how *they* thought I should begin my book.

"You could start with the story Don tells about being the first person to hear you sing," Daddy suggested.

Don had finished graduate work in New York at about the time Daddy became a regular on the *Arthur Godfrey* show, and he joined the fledgling Boone staff while he was waiting to be called into the army. He moved into an extra bedroom downstairs in my parents' house when it became apparent my father would be out of town singing during the time my mother was due to have her third child. Don was to be responsible for rushing my mother to the hospital. Actually, my father wasn't singing when I was born. He was playing golf.

"After Don called to tell me the good news, I went right back on the course." Daddy laughed. "I couldn't come home right away because I had another show to do that night. Besides, Debby, you were just another girl."

When the doctor came out looking for the father of a healthy, but squalling, new daughter, he mistook Don for Pat Boone.

"He told him how often and how much he enjoyed watching him on TV. He must have had a terrible television set," Daddy said.

Recently, Don had begun claiming that he'd put my footprint on a contract that first day in the hospital, but that it had taken him twenty-one years to find the right song for me to record.

We toyed with other ideas for the book, more playfully than seriously. Finally, Daddy got up from the table.

"Sorry, gang, I've still got some packing to do. And I want to get to bed as soon as possible. That plane leaves early tomorrow, and this may be the last good night's sleep we'll have for a long time."

The Summer Tour

The next day, Don and I got on a plane for Kentucky and the Golden Plate Awards presentation. A day later, we met Daddy in Morristown, New Jersey, to begin a tour that would last more than two months.

Morristown is a well-to-do community set in the hills about twenty-five miles due west of New York harbor. The intense green of the countryside was almost overwhelming to a westerner like me, more used to the brown of the Southwest. From Morristown, I learned, George Washington used to spy on British troop movements in New York with his telescope. Morristown had obviously gone to great pains to preserve its colonial flavor.

The decision to tour with my father had been reached some months before. I had been faced with a choice: to join another entertainer as his or her opening act or to accompany my father in the same capacity or as a twosome. Going with Daddy had two advantages. We were accustomed to working together, and we'd received a large number of invitations to perform together. On the other hand, we knew we would be criticized for riding on each other's coattails.

When I prayed about it—which was often—I knew I was supposed to go with Daddy. The tour would be my best preparation for solo performances later. Still, I struggled. Daddy and I could get on each other's nerves, even though our relationship had made significant progress since the spanking incident in Ohio two years earlier.

I had received inquiries about performing with Neil Sedaka, Tom Jones, and other well-known performers. I admired each of these men as first-rate performers. To turn my back on such opportunities was hard, but I knew that God seldom does things in a way that suits our opinions. I think it was the prophet Isaiah who said that His ways are not our ways.

Daddy and I had first been on stage alone together in December 1977 in El Paso, Texas. Don Henley and I had gathered up material and put together a twenty-minute show for me to perform alone. Dad and I also worked on a couple of songs to perform together. Daddy had not heard any of my part of the show except "You Light Up My Life." I was shaky at the thought not only of facing a live audience alone but also of what Daddy would say. It felt especially good when I walked offstage into the wings, and he grabbed me, hugged me, and told me I'd done a great job. He loved my choice of material and seemed surprised at the vocal ability I demonstrated.

After that, we made several appearances together at places like the Sahara Hotel in Las Vegas. The time was a season of growth for me in a number of ways. Not only was I growing more used to working with live audiences, I was also learning how to roll with the punches that reviewers dealt out. They were down on my dad and me for performing together, using lots of cheap shots about Daddy's "sagging" career being bolstered by the "meteoric" (distinctly implying "temporary") success of "You Light Up My Life." Happily, the audiences liked us much better than the reviewers. I was astounded at the number of standing ovations we received. The people were warm, generous, and loving.

Early June found Daddy and me working together at Lake Tahoe. In that one short month Gabri and I had our "significant talk," Albie Pearson encouraged us about our future, and Gabri and I traveled to Hawaii and the Tokyo Music Festival together.

With my arrival in Morristown on Saturday, June 24, however, I was locked into an eight-week, nonstop tour. The Morristown show was just a one-night stand, and so was our next performance, in Portland, Maine. Then we settled down for a week of concerts in upstate New York. After that, we were in Long Island, Toronto, Connecticut, and Rhode Island, also for a week each. I spent my week in New York with Gabri—which I'll tell about later—and then it was on the road again.

Many nights, after our performances, Daddy and I went jogging together. The weather was cool and peaceful. Sometimes we logged two or three miles together. Nothing distracted us from unwinding and having good talks.

Often, we talked about our careers, especially mine. I was wondering how long we'd go on performing together, so I tried to learn everything I could from my father. He handled audiences much better than I did, because he was comfortable onstage. I had to think hard about what I was going to say before going in front of an audience. Daddy just walked out and said whatever came to mind. Sometimes the words didn't make sense to anybody but himself, but he was so comfortable that no one thought he sounded awkward. If I started to stumble over my words, I could sense that everyone, including myself, was confused.

"The ability to talk to an audience comes with experience," Daddy told me. "Remember: when you do make mistakes, the audience hardly ever realizes it. I just continue as if nothing is wrong and most times they stay with you. They can tell when you're enjoying yourself, and that makes it easier for them to enjoy you. You do that pretty naturally anyway, Deb. You don't have that much to worry about."

"You couldn't have told me that back in El Paso in December," I chuckled.

"Well, I'll admit I was a little scared for you that night."

"Yeah. You were real nice to me that night. Now, tell me, what did you *really* think?"

"Like I said, I was nervous for you. I wasn't at all sure what would happen. But, honestly, your performance bowled me over. I actually got goosebumps. Some of your songs brought tears to my eyes."

"Really? You know what I remember from that night?"

"No, what?"

"When I took my first bow at the end, the hems of my silk pants were trembling. My whole body was shaking. That's how scared I was. I was sure the whole audience could see it, too."

"Well, they couldn't. And you know, it seems like performing gets easier for you every night."

"Yeah," I replied, pleased.

For years, whenever on tour, my father would take his guitar. Upstate New York was no exception. One afternoon, I went to his suite for an early dinner. There was the guitar case, yet unopened, half-hidden behind an easy chair.

"I'm going to learn to play it," Daddy insisted when I asked him why he always brought the guitar along.

"Sure," I teased. I'd seen the instrument come down the ramp of every plane we flew on. And I knew Dad would only touch it once or twice during the entire tour.

Few people realize that neither my father nor I can read music. We learn our songs by ear. Though we can peck out tunes on the piano, we can't play any instruments. Ever since he was my age, Daddy has visualized himself playing the guitar. So it was always with us; never completely out of sight, but. . . .

"I *am* going to learn to play the guitar," he insisted, and we both laughed.

Several days later, a disc jockey called my manager to ask if I could visit a local children's hospital. The little girl whose parents had contacted the disc jockey had purchased tickets to my performance months ahead of time. Now there wasn't any way she could come to see me because she was being treated for a recently discovered brain tumor.

"Debby's visit will mean everything to her," the disc jockey said when Don called him for more information.

Everywhere I went, it seemed children were attracted to me, especially those who were handicapped, sick, or dying. I wondered why, when I had only one hit record.

During the morning before I was to visit the girl, I asked the Lord, "What do You want me to do?"

I didn't know how old she was. Ten or eleven, I supposed. The prognosis was not promising. What could I offer her? I couldn't just go and say, "How are you? Good to see you," and then walk away. I didn't want it to be like that. I wanted my visit to mean something important to both of us. I began looking through the Bible, trying to find something special to pass on to her or a clue as to what I should do.

Shall I give her my Bible, the one Gabri gave me? I wondered. *Maybe that's the answer. I'll tell her to keep reading it and give her some Scripture references.*

But that idea didn't feel right. I was frustrated, completely at a loss. As I was getting ready to leave for the hospital, I found a box with a little coin in it that someone had given me the night before. The coin was engraved with a picture of Jesus and was intended to be a token of remembrance for Russian Christians from their friends outside the Iron Curtain. The gift was a simple physical reminder of the unity in prayer between people separated by distance. Without much thought, I put it into my purse, thinking it might somehow come in handy.

When I arrived at the hospital, I learned that the girl, Alison Zach, was only six years old and had been unable to open her eyes since a recent brain surgery. She would never have been able to read my Bible. Her father said she played my first album all the time and had asked her sisters to record my performance at the concert. Unfortunately, they had pushed the wrong buttons on the recorder and had nothing for her to hear.

When I walked into her room, Alison was lying quietly in her bed. A red incision showed where the doctors had tried to remove the tumor. Her head was shaved. She couldn't open her eyes, only flutter her eyelids. She was conscious, and her parents told her I was there. I took her hand and began talking to her. When I promised to send her an autographed copy of my new album, she barely responded. But when I said I was going to pray for her, her little hand, which had felt so light and lifeless, began to squeeze mine. She tried to open her eyes, but couldn't open them far enough to see me. My heart was aching for little Alison, but I knew crying wouldn't help anyone. Fighting tears and wanting desperately to do something, anything, that would bring some comfort to Alison and her family, I suddenly remembered the coin in my purse. I found it and pressed it into her hand.

"Somebody gave this to me last night," I told her, explaining what it symbolized. "When you pick this up and feel it, it will remind you that we're linked together. I'll be thinking about you and praying for you."

She didn't try to answer but just kept feeling the coin. I knew she understood. God had answered the prayer I had prayed earlier that morning. I kissed her goodbye and excused myself to visit the other children.

Eventually, I toured the entire hospital. In spite of their terrible illnesses, which included leukemia and various kinds of paralyses, the kids were all smiles. They kept calling my name, and many knew the words and music to my songs. Several nurses told me that one girl sang "You Light Up My Life" in her sleep. I went to her room to see her, wondering, *What is this, Lord? Why was I chosen to sing a song that has such a special effect on sick and handicapped children?*

By the end of the day I was completely drained, still questioning what it all meant.

My father and I went to another children's hospital the next day. The visit was limited to the intensive care unit. We saw so many sick, sick children, some losing their hair from cancer treatments, others confined in body casts. One tiny in-

fant, her chest covered with bandages, had recently under-
gone open-heart surgery. I began asking myself again, *What
good can I do?*

The clincher came when I was taken into a special room to
see the last child, another six-year-old girl. Her recent open-
heart surgery was complicated by a very bad kidney infec-
tion. There was little chance she would survive. She was
hooked up to an array of machines. Tubes ran up her nose
and down her throat and out from her little thin arms. Under-
neath all the paraphernalia was the most beautiful blonde
hair and blue eyes, but her skin was a dull, orangey yellow. I
knew I'd never forget the penetrating look she gave me—a
sign of recognition, a cry for help.

"We're Christians," her mother said. "Please pray for her."

The mother began to cry, and my mind shouted, *Why me?
What am I doing here?*

At that moment, Daddy walked into the room. I was glad
to see him.

"Daddy, these people would like us to pray for this little
girl."

"Sure, what is her name?" Daddy asked, turning to the
parents.

"Rachel," her father responded. The mother briefly described her critical condition.

"Dear Lord," Daddy began, his head bowed, "we ask for
Your mercy and grace for little Rachel. We thank You for the
faith of her parents. We see You as the victor today. Death
has no power here, because You died and rose again and are
seated in the place of all authority in the universe. We thank
You that You have given us the authority to use Your mighty
name, Jesus, to stand against the destruction of the enemy.
Father, today, in this place, at this time, we declare the
Lordship of Jesus Christ, and we speak life and health and
peace to Rachel. In the mighty name of Jesus, amen."

On the way out of the hospital, a girl came up to me and
asked me to pray for her sister who'd been in a coma for a
week. Nodding my promise, I hurried away.

Late that night, I called Gabri and broke down.

"I can't take this," I told him. "What if the whole ten-week tour is going to be nothing but my walking through hospitals, promising to pray for dying children? I mean, should I be laying hands on these kids and asking God to heal them on the spot?" I asked. "Would that be faith, or would I just be making a fool out of myself?"

"Remember what Dan told you when you were nervous about going on the *Tonight* show?" Gabri asked. He was referring to what my brother-in-law had told me about the Ark of the Covenant in the Bible.

The Ark of the Covenant was a beautiful piece of art. Skilled craftsmen had fashioned it from acacia wood, overlaid with gold. God had told Moses how to have it made after Israel escaped from Egypt through the parted Red Sea. The Ark was the special symbol of God's presence in their midst.

Centuries later, the Ark was captured by the Philistines (1 Samuel 4–6). They put the Ark in a room with their god, Dagon, and during the night, Dagon toppled over and fell onto the ground. In the morning, the Philistines went in and picked up their god and set him upright. The following day, they found Dagon on the ground again, bowing before the Ark of Jehovah, this time with his head and hands broken off.

"The box itself did nothing," Gabri reminded me, "but the glory of the Lord did everything."

Gabri was telling me that I was another dwelling place of the Holy Spirit. With the Holy Spirit in me, all I had to do was go where the Lord directed. He would always be with me, and it was His responsibility, not mine, to make things happen. The power of God didn't come from my own strength, but from His. My problem was that I'd been trying to do things on my own, acting as more than a vessel.

After Gabri had once again assured me that "if God is for me, who can be against me?" I said goodbye and fell asleep peacefully.

The tour with Daddy was a wonderful time—a learning experience. I was learning to love and respect my dad as never before. We were enjoying each other's company. There never was any real tension. We disagreed about what to do on stage when we performed together, and we had different tastes, but we handled these differences well. We both wanted to be fair to each other. Compromise came easily.

Each morning we set aside time to read the Bible and pray together. There was always plenty to pray about. Mom might have called with prayer requests from home. The children we met in the hospitals were, of course, important. Each day, we committed our work and other activities into His hands, asking for guidance and protection.

Sometimes, we got into conversations about marriage and my relationship with Gabri. Daddy shared from his own experiences with Mom, and that helped me better understand what was going on between Gabri and me.

Something else that was good for me to watch was how my father responded to reviews, a problem I've already mentioned. Sometimes a reviewer would be very hostile toward him, me, or both of us. One day, after reading some really mixed reviews, he told me, "You should never take reviews too seriously, good or bad. Each one is only one person's opinion. You can never rely on that to be the complete truth. If you get a bad review, it may be contradicted by the audience's good response. And even good reviews should be taken with a grain of salt. After all, you always see things that could have been improved or corrected every time you perform."

Some people particularly enjoyed my father's part of the show, others preferred mine. But almost everyone enjoyed watching us together. The Lord used us to help and encourage families. We heard comments and received letters all during the tour from people who said it was refreshing to see a father and daughter who loved each other and enjoyed each other's company. From time to time we received reports that fathers and daughters who were having trouble in their relationship had gone home after our show and decided to work things out between them. We heard from many families that they had had a renewal of love among themselves after they'd seen us. After going through such a hard time with my dad, I felt good knowing we were helping to restore broken relationships. Seeing that, I'm convinced, was one of the main reasons the Lord had us work together on that tour.

Young girls often told me, "It makes us feel good that you love your dad and get along with him." There's a general feeling among teenagers that it's not "in" to get along with one's parents. Those who do are often made to feel foolish if they want to express love or respect for their parents.

The following transcript condenses several interviews I had with members of the press that summer. It says some interesting things about my relationship with my folks.

Question: How have you liked working with your dad on the road?

Answer: I've been enjoying it. Being together really helps overcome the problem of loneliness on the road. We keep each other company. Besides, I learn a lot. We're close, and we have a great time together.

Question: But it wasn't always that way, was it? Weren't you pretty rebellious when you were younger?

Answer: Yeah—I don't know if it was anything that spectacular. I think it was a normal rebellious period in a young person's life, starting I guess, around the age of thirteen or fourteen. When you're in high school, the peer pressure gets to be very intense. You want to be like your friends and do what your friends do. I grew up in a very strict home, and my parents didn't let me do whatever I wanted to. They were very strict about certain things: whether we could wear makeup, how late we could stay out, with whom we could go out, and what kind of clothes we wore. Their rules were a constant embarrassment to me in front of my friends.

I started rejecting my parents and the rest of my family as being totally outdated and square. I wasn't anything like them and didn't want to be. I wanted to be like my friends and be accepted by them. So, I rebelled against my parents.

What they didn't want me to look like is how I tried to look every day. I wanted to be with people I knew they didn't like, and do things I knew they didn't want me to do. I wasn't at the extreme of being hopelessly addicted to drugs or having sex at the age of twelve, but I did go through a very rough time of feeling like I hated my parents.

Question: What do you think made you change finally? What really broke that rebellious period? Was it as simple as outgrowing it, or what?

Answer: Well, part of it was growing up. But I don't think I would have just grown out of it. I think if my parents had handled it any differently—if they had put me away in boarding school or if they had said, "We give up; you do what you want to do and learn your lessons the hard way," it would have been a different story. But they didn't do any of that. They were very strict and very consistent. Even when I was looking at them with hate in my eyes, they still didn't let me go where they thought I shouldn't be. I guess deep down a small part of me recognized their motive; they really loved me and were concerned about me. They never showed anything different. I'd get spankings, and I'd get punished, but I was always told every day, "We love you." After a spanking, they'd make me hug them, and sometimes that would make me the angriest—but when I really thought about it, or when I had to get down to the basics, I knew that a lot of my friends who were allowed to do things I wanted to do had parents who just really didn't care. Mine did care. They prayed for me. They wanted to be with me. I knew a lot of kids whose parents never spent any time with them. Those kids loved to come to my house to be with my folks. Something in that showed me I had something worth a lot more than just getting to stay out late.

Question: Do you have any advice for parents these days that might be going through what your parents went through with you?

Answer: Don't give up and never feel you are facing a hopeless situation. Trust the Lord. Maybe my parents didn't do everything perfectly, but they always turned situations over to the Lord each day. When they felt hopeless, they got on their knees and they prayed that the Lord would protect me, that He would show me eventually which way to go and lead me out of the bad things I was getting into.

And He did. Through a lot of different events, the Lord showed me that my parents really loved me and that they really loved Him. I realized that if I would just trust Him and be obedient to those in authority over me, He would work through them to work out my life in a way that I would be the happiest. It took a long time for me to see that and a lot of hating my parents and wanting to run away. But through their consistency and their love, I was turned around. I always knew they loved me. And that is something you can't run away from too long.

Question: Do you have any advice for kids that might feel the frustrations of growing up under peer pressure?

Answer: I guess if I had to sum it up in one phrase, it would be "Hang in there," no matter how frustrating things get. And if you have parents who love you, but just don't understand where you're at, remember they're trying. Help them by talking with them, not just shouting at them. And if you feel that your parents don't love you, remember that God does. He loves you very much. And He is able to change situations and people even when it seems impossible. Just make sure your attitude is right, and God will do the rest.

Question: One last question. Looking back, do you think you would raise your children in the same way as your parents raised you?

Answer: It's so funny to think about that. Five years ago, I often said, "I'll never do this to my children." But, as I compare the results of my life and my sisters' lives to my friends' whom I thought had it so great, I can't help but say that my parents did something right along the way. How they brought me up worked a lot better in the long run than the methods of those parents who let their kids do anything and go anywhere.

Most of those kids have no direction, no discipline, no sense of what commitment is. And I do. I know a lot about discipline, and I know a lot about commitment—sticking with something, even when the going gets rough. I'm grateful every day to my parents for raising me so I could learn those things. So, basically, I think I would raise my kids in the same way. And I know I'll be hearing my kids say, "I'll never do this to my kids!" But, I hope, as another generation passes, they'll make the same choices I've made.

I need to back up now to that first week in August, in the midst of the tour, when I visited Gabri and his father in New York.

New York

As I looked out my window in the descending jet and saw the New York skyline in the distant haze, I got a little nervous. So much of my relationship with Gabri centered around me and my family. After Gabri and my parents became close, we spent a great deal of time with them at my house. The surroundings were so comfortable that the location became a habit.

I had dated Gabri for almost a year before I went to his mother's home for dinner. Rosemary Clooney, who is well-known for her good cooking as well as for her singing, finally took it upon herself to invite me after Gabri failed to suggest it. Since then, she and I have shared a lot of great times together. We've found we have several things in common.

For one, our careers had similar beginnings. She'd first sung with her sister Betty. Later, she, like me, had her first hit when she was about twenty-one years old. As we have gotten better acquainted, we've shared several other mutual experiences, and her advice based on her years of experience as an entertainer has been of great benefit to me.

Gabri's father, Jose Ferrer, was still sort of a mystery. Since he lived in New York, I had not spent much time with him before. Now, I was going to stay at his apartment during my vacation, and I wasn't quite sure what to expect.

Gabri met my flight and drove me to where his father lived in midtown Manhattan. The apartment was high up in a beautiful old building with large, open rooms and seventeen-foot ceilings. The residence occupied two stories. As I unpacked in my room, I was careful to keep everything in some semblance of order.

Soon after Gabri and I began talking with his father, I got over my nervousness. Jose is a wonderfully warm, quick-witted person with a tremendous passion for knowledge. He seems as fascinated with life as anyone I've ever met.

Gabri and I went along to an acting class Jose was teaching and watched several girls perform a scene from a play. Noticing the high level of intensity as one of the girls acted out a very emotional part, I told Gabri I thought she was very good. I was embarrassed when I discovered that he and his father thought she was awful. *Oh, well, so much for my acting sense,* I thought to myself.

Later, Jose told a wonderful story about how another teacher used a big blackboard to show what it took to be a successful actor. He drew a number of boxes and labeled them with such ingredients as knowledge of theatrical history, voice projection, movement, facial expressiveness, interpretation, and all the other technical skills. In the center of the diagram, the teacher left one large box empty. When he finished explaining all the other boxes, a student finally asked about the empty one.

"That's the most important," the teacher said. "You may study and learn everything else, but without that special nameless quality represented by the empty box, you can't be a really good actor. And if you have that special thing, you don't need any of the others."

Gabri and I saw five or six Broadway shows during the next three or four days, sometimes going to matinees and sometimes to evening performances. We ate at different restaurants every night, all of them famous for good food. We were having a wonderful time.

I found myself experiencing mixed emotions, though, especially when I was alone at night, reflecting on all the excitement of the day. It was great fun, but I was allowing myself to be intimidated by it all. Jose was so smart and seemed to know something about everything. Listening to him talk was always stimulating, but I found myself afraid to contribute anything, in case I might say something foolish. Every time I was in the apartment and saw his vast supply of books, I couldn't help but wonder if I had read even ten books in the four years since I had been out of high school.

My lack of book learning wasn't all that bothered me. I was seeing so much talent exhibited around me that I was beginning to wonder if my ability was worth much at all. I had achieved a lot of success at a young age, but there were plenty of successful people who didn't have much talent. I had always thought of myself as being very serious about my singing career; yet I had never even learned to read music. I suppose I was feeling I had wasted a lot of time in my life. Worst of all, I wasn't sure I had enough initiative and discipline to try to catch up. Such feelings were strange to me. I felt like a country girl coming to the city for the first time. Having grown up in a show business family in Hollywood, I never thought I would find myself in that position.

I decided I needed a little moral support, and I called Donna in Los Angeles.

"Are you having a great time?" she asked.

"Oh, it's been incredible! We've been so busy, seeing great plays and, of course, eating," I said happily.

"How is it working out for you, staying in the apartment?" Donna knew I had been a little apprehensive about staying with Jose, since I didn't know him very well.

"It's been going fine. I love Gabri's dad, and he's been so nice, but. . . ." I proceeded to tell her about my insecurities.

After listening to me lament for a while, Donna interrupted:

"Join the club! Try living with my dad for a while."

Donna's father is Stan Freberg, the ingenious humorist. Famous for his satirical records of the 1960s, he is also a very successful writer.

"I'm supposed to be working on a writing career, and I can

hardly spend an hour reading *or* writing," Donna confided.

We both laughed. One of the great things about our friendship is that we always seem to relate strongly to each other's feelings. We decided we would have to work on our self-discipline if these things were truly important to us.

The vacation in New York proved to be very positive in Gabri's and my relationship. I was seeing a totally different side of him when he was with his father, in this environment. While I was wallflowering, he was really coming out of himself, revealing bits of information on art, history, architecture, and many other things I didn't know he was interested in. In fact, I had often wondered if Gabri had many interests. I was the one who could talk forever about what I did during the day and what I wanted to do in the future; he was always very quiet about himself. I assumed he was more or less passionless, and I often worried that that would soon be a problem in our relationship. I was the kind of person who experienced constant emotional highs and lows, and I thought his steady temperament meant he just didn't care about anything the way I did.

I couldn't have been more wrong. I now realized that he cared about many things and not only would help me expand my horizons but would be a leveling influence in my life. In many ways, he was ten times more passionate than I. The problem was, I hadn't seen his intensity because I'd had little interest in what interested him.

"Do you remember that conversation we had in your living room when I accused you of being passionless and uninteresting?" I asked.

He nodded, beginning to smile.

"Well, I just never had a chance to see you like this before. I didn't know how many different things excite you."

After that, Gabri's interests were contagious. I started noticing the differences in architecture, color schemes, and proportions, the subtleties in brush strokes on canvas—so many things I'd never looked for before.

Gabri and Jose took me next door to visit an artist who'd

done over three hundred covers for the *New Yorker*. Very quiet and very proper, the old man lived on the top floor of a building similar to Jose's. The ceilings were covered with skylights. Huge windows ran from floor to ceiling along two walls of the main room. There appeared to be no other lighting, but I could easily see every line and shade of the paintings that were everywhere. The technical perfection was nearly as amazing as the tremendous feeling evident in each work.

I followed the artist, Gabri, and Jose from room to room, while they discussed each of his works in detail. This time I didn't mind being left out of the conversation. I was interested in listening to Gabri's contributions and in watching the enthusiasm lighting up his face. I felt very proud of him.

One of the highlights of my vacation came when Jose took us to lunch at the Players Club. The four-story mansion was once the home of Edwin Booth, the famous American actor who quit the stage after his brother, John Wilkes Booth, assassinated President Lincoln.

While we were eating, Jose told about a time he was walking around the club with one of the directors, looking at the many busts of famous actors and playwrights that were on display. Seeing one he didn't recognize, Jose asked who it was. "That's you," the director answered, pointing out that the bust had been there for nearly twenty years.

Gabri shares his father's ability to blend pride with humility. Recognizing that, along with my new understanding of the scope and depth of Gabri's interests, I felt much more comfortable with our relationship. Yet, one thing still bothered me quite a bit. Sometimes I resented Gabri's seemingly careless, passive attitude about money. Even though we certainly didn't go first class all the time we were running around New York, Gabri spent all the money he'd received as birthday presents. I was glad to help pay the bills occasionally, but it frustrated me to think that Gabri never worried about setting anything aside for the future. He actually seemed to think that money was "no big deal."

Considering the fact that Gabri didn't have a definite career, I worried about his role definition if we were to get married. At the time, he was teaching several Bible classes, working in ceramics, drawing and painting, and attending Pepperdine College. Though he sometimes leaned toward the ministry, he had no specific goals. The thought of people calling Gabri a "freeloader" scared me. I assumed that such a situation would be difficult, if not downright impossible, for the male ego to tolerate. Visualizing his old Volkswagen parked next to my new Mercedes, I wondered if he'd be able to adjust to the omnipresent symbols of my success.

The week with him in New York helped ease my worries some. I learned that Gabri was confident the Lord would lead him into the right profession. He wasn't worried about when that would happen. His God-given humility and lack of false pride allowed him to support me in so many other ways that money was, indeed, "no big deal." I, too, was beginning to learn to relax . . . but I was a long way from learning to make a deep and lasting commitment, as the events of the coming months would soon show.

Learning Love

Gabri and I were getting along well enough, but I was still unsure about our relationship. For some reason I found it very frustrating and unfulfilling. I couldn't see much ambition in Gabri. He'd had several offers to become a pastor or teacher that would have allowed him to continue with school. He turned them all down, saying he wasn't sure what he wanted to do.

I tried to imagine our getting married, moving into a house that I had paid for, and living entirely off what I earned. I could not believe that Gabri could allow me to do that and simultaneously maintain any kind of self-respect.

Furthermore, there was a growing lack of stimulation in our relationship. Gabri seemed to be unconcerned about how he looked when he was around me, and I certainly didn't care what I looked like around him. I liked the fact that Gabri accepted me in whatever state he found me, but on the other hand I missed feeling the need, at least on occasion, to look beautiful for him. More than that, I missed his feeling any need to impress me. I felt like the honeymoon was over before it had ever begun.

One afternoon I had an autograph party at one of the largest record stores in Los Angeles. The party was being given and promoted by a popular radio station in the area. Gabri knew I would be there and came by with his brother Miguel to say hello. I was busy signing albums when I looked up and saw Gabri walking into the store. I was horrified. I had never seen him looking so awful. He was wearing old jeans and an even older Mexican sweater. He had on a cap which pushed his ears straight out and his hair was filthy. To top it off, he had not shaved for at least three or four days.

I toyed with the idea of pretending I'd never seen him before in my life, but the photographers who were there recognized him as soon as he said hello to me. Of course, to my dismay, they made us pose together for some pictures. I shuddered to think where those pictures would turn up.

The incident made me realize how much I cared what other people thought about Gabri. I found myself comparing him to other singers' and actresses' boyfriends. I wanted the public to be impressed by my choice. I often felt guilty about having these thoughts, but that didn't change my attitude.

All of this put me in a very vulnerable position when I worked with attractive and talented men.

Gabri and I were not officially engaged, but we were planning to marry eventually. I found myself feeling uncomfortable with that commitment when, usually at the start of a new job, I would meet some new guy who looked pretty attractive. Then, as the attraction grew, I would conclude that my love for Gabri was not strong enough to be considering marriage.

If I sound overtly evasive about the experiences I'm about to describe, it is not because I have anything to hide; but the other persons involved are entitled to their privacy. Also, the details of these relationships are not pertinent. What is pertinent are the conclusions I came to at the end of it all.

Not long after that autograph party, I became seriously involved with another man.

When I say "seriously involved," I mean that in a relatively short period of time I developed such a close relationship with him that I was severely tempted to break things off with Gabri. I knew that would be wrong, because I knew deep inside the Lord meant for us to marry someday. But knowing right and doing right are two different things, especially when emotions are involved. I procrastinated and deliberated until the last possible moment, making the situation more painful for everyone concerned when I finally did what I knew I had to do from the start.

Meanwhile, Gabri knew something unusual was going on but wasn't sure of the problem. He handled my evasiveness about what was wrong with remarkable grace. I wouldn't have blamed him if he had given up on me altogether, but he didn't. He was more understanding than I ever could have hoped for.

After several weeks of tolerating my strange behavior, including an obvious reluctance to spend time with him, Gabri called. "I really miss you and want to see you. Let's get together tonight over at my house."

I sensed his insecurity and confusion. Even though I wasn't ready to talk about anything yet, I thought I'd better see him right away before he got more suspicious.

When I arrived, there was a fire in the fireplace and music playing in the background. Instead of encouraging me to relax and enjoy our evening together, this romantic atmosphere made me feel awful. I stood there a moment thinking, *How can I do this, acting as if nothing were wrong?*

I tried to steer our conversation away from the real problem. When Gabri said, "You seem upset about something. Is anything wrong?" I answered vaguely "No, not really. I'm just confused about a couple of things."

"Like what?"

"Just don't worry about it, okay? I'm fine, really."

"I want to help you deal with whatever problem it is you're trying to hide from me."

That made me feel worse. I was sure if he really knew what the problem was, he wouldn't want to help me. More likely, he probably wouldn't want to see me again.

"Look, Gabri, it doesn't concern you. It's just something I have to work through on my own. I'll be fine in a couple of days." I finally left, feeling horrible.

Three days later I tried seeing him again. Over dinner, Gabri asked me if I was feeling better.

"Yes," I lied, knowing I hadn't answered the question he was trying to ask.

When I remained evasive, Gabri began acting coldly toward me. I responded the same way. Soon we were *both* building walls between us. Our remarks became cutting. We finally stopped talking altogether.

Riding silently in the car on the way home, I realized that if I kept this up I would destroy a longtime relationship with a guy I really loved. Was that what I wanted to do?

Besides, treating him this way, just because I was having a hard time dealing with myself, wasn't right. I was sure I was making him react in a way that he didn't like any better than I did. I decided to say something—but I still didn't want to tell him everything.

"I'm sorry I'm acting so weird. Just kind of bear with me until I work some things out."

Unfortunately for me, Gabri wanted to know specifically what was wrong. In response, I began listing the things that frustrated me about him: no ambition, no career, and no need to look good for me. Yet, every time I told him a little bit more about what I thought was wrong with our relationship, he insisted that there was more. Finally, I ran out of complaints.

"If we're ever going to solve our problems, we've got to be completely honest with each other," he said. "Why do I feel there's something you're hiding from me? Is there another guy?"

"Don't even guess . . . don't worry about . . . yes," I finally admitted and began telling him everything.

Gabri was shocked by my answer. His question had been a shot in the dark, and when he realized he was right, he was hurt. I felt bad for putting him through this. I reached out to hold his hand, but he pulled away.

"Are you still seeing him?"

"No. I told him I had to try to make my relationship with

you work. I didn't mean to get involved. It just happened."

"It doesn't 'just happen.' You have to *want* it to happen at some point."

"Don't be so self-righteous," I said defensively. "Haven't you ever found yourself attracted to someone else?"

"Of course, I have. The same thing happened to me about a year ago," he said.

While he was committed to me, he had been attracted to another girl at college. There were times when he thought an important relationship with her might develop, but he stopped their friendship before it even had a chance to deepen.

At first, I couldn't imagine Gabri going through something like I'd been through. I had never been aware that he even noticed other girls. I had never been jealous of anyone he spent time with, although I had made him jealous several times. I realized I figured Gabri would always be there, no matter what.

"In a way I'm glad it happened to you, too," I said. "I've handled things badly, but at least now I think you can understand what I've been going through."

That night Gabri and I communicated better than ever; we talked until after 2:00 in the morning.

"We can never make our relationship work if we don't express our feelings," he said. "When something is bothering you, tell me. Don't let it build up inside."

"Then what about your life?" I asked. "Doesn't it bother you that your life hasn't taken any direction—that you don't have a career?"

"Now, wait a second," Gabri interrupted. "When I got out of high school, I had an art scholarship to USC and could have gone right to college. I didn't, because after I became a Christian I felt the Lord wanted me to go to Bible school instead. Later, I wanted to go to Israel and Europe. That trip was important. I was on my own and had plenty of time to grow up in a lot of ways. After coming home, I enrolled at Pepperdine College as an art major—because I believed that was the Lord's will. Even though I've been offered good jobs since then, I'm staying at Pepperdine because I believe that's where the Lord wants me to be."

Gabri paused to see if I understood what he was saying, but I made no comment.

Quietly, he asked, "What would you do differently if you were in my place?"

I didn't know what to say. I couldn't argue with his analysis of his situation. Like myself, he knew the Lord had plans for him; he just didn't know what all of them were yet. He didn't lack ambition or concern about the future. Everything Gabri had done since graduating from high school had been what he thought the Lord wanted him to do. He believed that he was exactly where the Lord wanted him to be now. Did I want him to please me or the Lord?

What Gabri said next really turned my head around: "Do you *really* believe God *gave* you your career?"

I resented the implications and immediately said, "Of course, I do."

"Then you'll remember that you had nothing to do with your success. You didn't even write the song. And it's not as if you spent years working in small clubs, trying to make a name for yourself. That song was dropped right into your lap. Then, within a month's time, you had a hit single at the top of the charts, and everything began to happen at once."

He was absolutely right. I couldn't take any credit for my recent success; even my musical talent was a gift. My whole career was the Lord's doing and had nothing to do with any planning on my part. I needed to remember that whatever Gabri did in the future was also in God's control.

My feelings toward Gabri changed that evening when I saw how he responded to the fact that I had compromised my commitment to him. He was able to control his jealousy and try to work out the problem. That showed unselfish love, not a love based only on emotions.

I was getting ready to do a rodeo in Kansas City with my dad, and I asked Gabri to come with us. We spent that week praying together, spending long hours deep in conversation, and enjoying each other's company. We were trying hard to strengthen our relationship so that neither of us would be tempted to bail out again. I felt very good about our time together. There was a new openness between us.

I wish I could say I learned my lesson after all that, but I didn't. Shortly after I returned home, I found myself tempted by yet another man, this time more strongly than before.

Instead of thinking things through rationally and cutting off the relationship before I got too involved, I let my feelings take over once again. I was amazed by my actions. After all Gabri and I had gone through, trying so hard to work things out, how could I be feeling so strongly about someone else? I remember thinking, *I didn't go out looking for this! It just happened.* Then Gabri's answer came back to me: "It doesn't 'just happen.' You have to *want* it to at some point."

I rationalized that what he said was not true in this case. I truly wanted things to work out with Gabri. Why would I want to get involved with someone else?

The emotional struggle became unbearably intense. In one way, I wanted to pull away from this man who was so appealing and yet so wrong for me. Instead, I would find myself agreeing to meet for dinner or lingering after a rehearsal to talk just a while longer. Physically the relationship never got beyond embracing and kissing, but I enjoyed that so much that I didn't want to stop it.

All of this culminated in a major inner crisis when my parents were briefly out of town. They arrived home one evening while I was out having dinner with this man. I didn't get in until nearly 2:00 in the morning, and I went straight to bed.

I had just turned out the light when my mother slipped into the room. "Deb, are you awake?" she whispered.

"Yeah. Good to have you home. Did you and Daddy have a good trip?"

"Oh, just fine. But I really wanted to check on you. Is everything all right?"

I sensed concern in her voice. Suddenly I realized how very

much alone I felt. What a mess I had gotten myself into! That was all I needed.

"Not really, I guess." I poured out the whole story, omitting nothing.

She listened patiently until I was finished. "Honey," she said, "I think I understand what's going on. I came in here to ask how you were doing because I couldn't get to sleep after we went to bed. I was lying there praying when I had a distinct mental impression of your face. You were crying out for help and then I saw why. Your whole body had become nothing more than a skeleton. You didn't have an ounce of strength to help yourself. I asked the Holy Spirit to show me what the picture meant, and it occurred to me that you were in a battle without spiritual armor. All your strength, spiritual and physical, was gone."

"That's really how I feel." I began to cry, and she held me in her arms. After that we talked and prayed a while longer, and then I fell asleep. As I prayed during the following weeks, I changed. The temptations grew less intense. As they did, I began to see clearly how I had toyed with the feelings of others, entirely for my own selfish desires. I had actually entertained the idea that it was impossible to make a serious and lasting commitment to one person, because I might later meet someone else who was better suited to me.

As I looked at the situation more realistically, I recognized that Gabri was right. I had not gone out looking for another man, but when I began to feel strongly about someone whom I knew felt the same way about me, instead of refusing to get involved further, I pursued the relationship as far as I wanted it to go. I wish I had realized sooner that using someone just for the pleasures along the way is never worth it; the price is always too high. I ended up frustrated, confused, and guilty of having inflicted pain on people I cared about. Even worse, my actions had negated any positive spiritual effect I might otherwise have had on the two men involved.

Through all of this, by the grace of God, Gabri's love for me remained constant. He was able somehow to love me, despite his feelings of mistrust and resentment for all I had put him through. He even remained objective enough to look for ways he might have provoked me to look for someone else to fulfill my needs. I explained to him that I often felt he didn't need me. I knew he loved me, but I thought that with or without me his life would virtually be the same. When I found two guys who thought I was wonderful and who seemed to need me very much, I responded readily. Gabri and I spent much time talking about our individual strengths and weaknesses and how we really did need each other. At the end of it all, we found we loved each other more than ever.

I was learning the first truth about love. The lesson can be stated simply, but it is not simple to learn: Love is a matter of choice, not of feelings. I'm still working on that truth. The matter rests in my will, not in my emotions or feelings. I don't have to be afraid when I feel attracted to other men. I need only to discipline myself and take the matter to the Lord, not getting preoccupied with the attraction and not letting it build into anything more. I recall the Scripture that reads: "No temptation has overtaken you that is not common to man. God is faithful, and he will not let you be tempted beyond your strength, but with the temptation will also provide the way of escape, that you may be able to endure it" (1 Corinthians 10:13).

My attraction to two men who "needed" me had been pretty self-serving. Yet Gabri had loved me, even at times when there was little there to love. C. S. Lewis put it very well:

> We are all receiving Charity. There is something in each of us that cannot be naturally loved. It is no one's fault if they do not so love it. Only the lovable can be naturally loved. You might as well ask people to like the taste of rotten bread or the sound of a mechanical drill. We can be forgiven, and pitied, and loved in spite of it, with Charity; no other way. All who have good parents, wives, husbands, or children, may be sure that at some

times—and perhaps at all times in respect of some one particular trait or habit—they are receiving Charity, are loved not because they are lovable but because Love Himself is in those who love them (*The Four Loves*, p. 183).

I had been the object of love which came from God through Gabri. God called me to express that sort of love to others, rather than the momentary good feeling that came when someone told me they needed me.

I finally realized that nothing was ever going to work out with Gabri until I made a once-and-for-all commitment to him, to be with him through whatever was going to happen. With that decision, my fear of commitment began to diminish. Commitment to Gabri was a choice, just as it would be my choice not to get involved with anyone else, nor let feeling and desires snowball anymore. The more I realized these things, the closer Gabri and I became. I would make the right choices and my heart would follow, not lead.

The Engagement

In the fall of 1978 I had accepted an invitation to do some acting. I got the lead female role in the lovely story of "The Gift of the Magi" by O. Henry, which aired on December 21. My parents, Gabri, and I gathered around the TV set in the den that evening to watch my debut. I was terribly nervous. I kept looking away from the screen, checking to see if the others were enjoying themselves and hoping they approved of my performance.

As soon as the film ended, I left the room to take a congratulatory telephone call. When I returned, I noticed Gabri talking secretively with my parents. He was showing them something, but as I approached, he put whatever it was away and they all began talking about how much they liked the film.

During the last days before Christmas, I sensed that something extraordinary was happening. Donna and I planned to exchange presents early on Christmas Eve. When I got to her house, I asked her if she knew what was up.

"No. Why?" Donna asked, looking up from wrapping a present.

"I have this sneaking suspicion that Gabri's going to ask me to marry him tonight."

"What makes you think that?" Donna kept on wrapping the present.

She knew Gabri and I had talked about marriage, but he'd

160

never asked me—never even implied that we should think about it anytime soon.

"But now there are a number of things. . . ." I began listing them for her. "Gabri said he wanted me to come over to his house and open presents alone with him later tonight. There was something in his voice. . . . I don't know. And then there are my parents. Every time my mother looks at me now, she smiles. Daddy does too. They have that 'we-know-a-secret' look in their eyes."

When the reality that maybe I wasn't just imagining things hit Donna, she dropped the package she was working on and said, "What are you going to do?"

"I don't know. Right now, I'm panicking," I said, as other clues flashed through my mind.

"Let's not worry about it now," Donna said.

But when it was time for me to go, we became very serious. Sitting cross-legged on the floor, we hugged each other.

"What *am* I going to do?" I asked, definitely choked up. "I didn't think it would happen so soon. I just don't feel prepared."

"I don't think people like you or me ever feel totally prepared," Donna said. "That's where trusting the Lord comes in."

I nodded, then I began to laugh. "What if I'm panicking over nothing? What if Gabri doesn't ask me?"

Telling me to run—not walk—back to her house if I did get engaged, Donna led me to the front door.

Later that night, Gabri and I sat next to the little Christmas tree I had set up for him near the window in his room. Gabri handed me a pillow made in the shape of a daisy with removable petals.

"You can say, 'He loves me, he loves me not,' if you ever get to feeling insecure," Gabri explained, laughing as he showed me how it worked.

We opened gifts from my parents next. The one from my mother to me was a porcelain figure of the angel Gabriel.

With it was a typewritten explanation of what my mother thought the name "Gabriel" should mean to us, taken from a Bible dictionary.

GABRIEL

"Gabriel" means "man of God" or "God has shown Himself mighty." The angel Gabriel was called a man in Daniel 8:16 and 9:21. He functions to reveal that which is to come in the day of judgment, to make known a vision (Daniel 8:17), and to give understanding and wisdom (Daniel 9:22).

Other references show him to be both revealer and bringer of reassurance (Luke 1:11–20 and Judges 13:3).

In Luke 1:26–38, he announced the birth of a son to Mary. He is one who stands in the presence of God (Luke 1:19) and can therefore reassure, "Do not be afraid . . . you have found favor with God" (Luke 1:30).

An allusion is made to Gabriel in Revelation 8:3, though not by name, as one of those who stands before God. In a characteristically Hebraic sense, where the messenger is, there God is fully present. Gabriel acts as a messenger before he is understood as an angel, revealing the graciousness and powerful purpose of the One who sends him.

Along with my mother's present to Gabri, there was a similar description of my biblical namesake, Deborah, taken from a book about women in the Bible.

DEBORAH

Occasionally, a strong-minded and unique woman breaks in upon human history and by her exploits leaves the impact of her personality upon events and secures for herself an imperishable honor.

Gifted with superior spiritual, mental, and physical powers to leave her mark upon the annals of time was Deborah, whom God raised up and endowed with a remarkable personality and varied gifts for the deliverance of His distressed and defeated people. A woman of unusual attainments, Deborah carved out an enviable niche for herself. With characteristic resoluteness, she occupied several positions.

She was a wife. In his quieter way, her husband was the encourager of Deborah in all her activities. Although not called by God to the same task as his wife's, he was illuminative in his own way. Behind the scenes he was as good and conspicuous in faith as the woman he loved, and in whose glory he was content to bask. Deborah would never have become the dazzling figure she was, had she not had the love, sympathy, advice, and encouragement of a husband who was happy to ride in the second chariot.

She was a prophetess. Deborah sat stately in person with her dark, penetrating, prophetic eyes and poured out wisdom and intuition, as well as inspiration. . . . Deborah was an effective agitator who stirred up Israel's concern about its low spiritual condition.

She was a leader. She dispensed righteousness, justice, and mercy.

She was a warrior. Having fought with words, she went forth to throw off the oppressor's yoke with swords, and what a fighter this patriotic and inspired heroine proved to be. The dauntless spirit of Deborah did not quail. True, tremendous odds were against them, but Deborah had God as her ally.

She was a poetess. Deborah could not only prophesy, arouse, lead, and fight, but also write. Out of the contest and conquest came the moral purification of the nation, and the inspiring genius of it was a woman daring and dynamic in the leadership of her nation.

Deborah—prophetess, leader, warrior, and poetess. Her song is immortal because her life was dedicated to God.

She was a maternal figure. Above all of her remarkable gifts was her trust in God, which is ever the source of any woman's highest adornment. Hers was a brilliant career, because of a heart that was fixed on God. She served God to the limit of her ability and capacity. She went out to fight the Lord's battles with a song on her lips and the Word in her hand.

Gabri and I were deeply touched. "These are perfect," we agreed.

Then Gabri said, "I have one more gift."

He handed me a little blue velvet box. Breathless, I opened it.

"Oh, Gabri," I gasped, and quickly snapped the box shut.

Seeing the ring inside, I was completely overwhelmed for a moment. I knew I had to make the biggest decision of my life.

Hugging him, I said, "Earlier tonight, I told Donna, 'If the Lord wants me to marry Gabri soon, He will need to let me know by shooting down an arrow with a note attached.' I guess my mother's letter was that note."

"What are you doing next year?" he asked.

"Next year?" I could hear my voice quavering. "Have you talked to my parents about all this?"

"Uh-huh." Gabri smiled and began telling me about everything that had been going on.

By the middle of December, he still hadn't figured out what to get me for Christmas. One night he asked his mother for ideas. She went to her jewelry box and found an unset diamond.

"How about this?" Rosemary suggested. "You can have it set in a necklace or. . . ."

She didn't mention an engagement ring, but Gabri was suddenly beginning to realize the timing was right. So, he bought the diamond from his mother with that in mind. The next step was to talk to my parents. He got frantic thinking about that.

How do you ask Pat Boone for his daughter's hand? he wondered.

Still thinking about it, he showed the diamond to my parents the night we watched "The Gift of the Magi" together. My mother had just asked him how he intended to use it when I came back into the room. The next day, still wanting to know the answer, she called Gabri.

"We've got to have lunch," she said.

"When?"

"Now. I'll meet you at the Hamburger Hamlet on Sunset in fifteen minutes," my mother said.

With barely enough time to pray for help, Gabri rushed to meet my mother. He was more excited than worried. He felt the Lord was encouraging him. After five minutes of general chit-chat, my mother asked him about the diamond.

"What are you going to do with it?"

"Funny you should ask," he said, smiling back at her. "I want to give it to Debby set in an engagement ring."

"Why haven't you talked to Pat and me?" my mother wanted to know.

"Because I have been scared to death."

"Well, you've got to talk to Pat immediately. I already feel good about the idea. I think Debby needs your spiritual covering." My mother got up from the table and started to leave. "I'll get you and Pat together this afternoon. I'll call you."

Wanting to hurry back to his house to wait for my mother's call, Gabri was more than a little frustrated to find that the clutch cable in his V.W. had snapped. He had to call my mother and ask her to come back and get him.

When she pulled up in front of the restaurant for the second time that day, she told Gabri, "I've already talked to Pat, and he'll pick you up at your place at 4:30."

Preparing for the big meeting, Gabri showered and shaved, cutting himself for the first time in months. Five minutes before Daddy was scheduled to arrive, Gabri went out in front of his house and sat on the curb. At exactly 4:30, a green Rolls Royce came cruising down the street. It was one of the few times Gabri could remember my father's being on time.

As soon as Gabri got into the car, Daddy said, "I've

pumped Shirley, and I think I know what we're going to talk about."

"Sitting there waiting for you, I thought maybe you had figured it out," Gabri said.

"I guess so, but I've never looked forward to a conversation as much as I have this one," Daddy told him. "Shirley and I have been watching happily. It's never been a question of what was going to happen eventually, just when. I have full confidence that you two are tailor-made—the Lord's custom fit—for each other."

The next day, December 23, Gabri realized he had less than twenty-four hours to get the diamond set in a ring. He called Tiffany's, who sent him to the jeweler who did their work. The man promised to have the ring ready the next day, but when Gabri went to pick it up, the man had left for the day, Christmas Eve. He'd left word for Gabri to meet him at his house in Santa Monica.

"So, while you were visiting Donna, I was rushing across the city to get your ring," Gabri said, finishing his story and pointing to the blue velvet box.

Wearing my ring, I helped Gabri open a present that my mother had told him to save until the very last. It was a pair of delicately handpainted glasses. The card read:

> For Gabri,
>   To celebrate this "special day" with the "special person" of your choice.
>   With love,
>   Pat and Shirley

Gabri was delighted and astonished. "You know," he said, "your mother told me she picked out that gift months ago and that the card was written and sealed in its envelope last August."

"It's the same with the descriptions of what our names

mean," I said. "My mother must have worked on those for a long time, too."

"It's incredible how the Lord can orchestrate a series of events," Gabri said.

First we told Gabri's mother, who was ecstatic at the news. Then we went to Donna's house. Already in bed and nearly asleep, she was flabbergasted when we burst into her room about midnight.

"I know, I know. Just tell me one thing—when do I lose my best friend?"

At my house, those who were asleep were awakened in a hurry. Everyone gathered in Laury's room, recounting what had happened.

"It's 1:00," someone noticed. "It's Christmas."

Later, after Gabri had left and as I was on my way to bed, I heard my father talking on the phone to Gabri's mother.

"You know, for years Shirley and I have been praying that God would provide the perfect mate for each of our girls, including Debby," he was telling her. "And all the while, there was Gabri, growing up just a few blocks away."

Karey

As the new year began, I was glad to have my relationship with Gabri basically resolved and on course. By confining myself in commitment to him, I was finding new freedom in my work and in other pursuits. This freedom led to one experience that I particularly want to tell about.

Early in February I had just gotten home from a stand in Las Vegas. I found in my mail a letter from the mother of the little girl, Alison, whom I had visited in the hospital in New York about eight months before.

> Elma, New York
> January 31, 1979
>
> Dear Debby,
>
> Although this thank you is *very long* overdue, I felt the need, nevertheless, to send it to you and to express what we feel for you.
>
> You may not remember us, but I think you will after I refresh your memory. . . . You visited our daughter, Alison, at Roswell Park Memorial Institute where she was a patient. She was ill with a brain tumor. As you may have gathered by now, if you've looked at the enclosed card, Ali died on December 10.
>
> She did get better than she was when you saw her. If you recall, she was rather unresponsive—or rather, she appeared to be.

After Ali came home in August, she told us about many things that happened while she was in the hospital which we did not realize that she was aware of. One of these was your visit. We shall always treasure the beautiful medallion you gave to Alison. One of the inscriptions, "I can do all things through Christ who strengthens me," was really a source of comfort and strength during the course of Ali's illness. Now when the days seem so dark and the nights too long without Ali, these words are something to hang onto.

The beautiful album you promised to send came shortly after Alison's birthday. In fact, it came after the first weekend Ali was allowed to spend at home. We were just preparing to return to the hospital on Monday afternoon when the postman delivered it. It was such a wonderful surprise and perfect timing. . . .

I must tell you, Debby, that Alison's *favorite* song was, of course, "You Light Up My Life." . . . Our church choir sang this song at her funeral mass. It was so appropriate for our darling little angel. It's *her* theme song, as well as yours. In fact, everyone who really knows Ali associates you with her. I spoke to Ali's doctor on the phone a couple of weeks ago, and he said he was watching TV the night before and saw you and heard the song and he immediately thought of Alison. . . .

Well, Debby, I'll close for now wishing you many blessings and continued success in your career and life. We've read about your engagement, and we wish you the best of everything and much happiness. You've given our sweetheart Alison and us, as well as so many others, so much happiness and pleasure, *you* deserve the *best.* You're so sweet and sincere. I hope you never change. May God bless you always.

Sincerely,
Sylvia Zach

P.S. One more thing I'd like to relate to you, Debby. On my birthday, Sept. 20, John brought out his tape recorder and recorded Ali singing "Happy Birthday" to me.

Then she surprised us all and sang, "You Light Up My Life" and said "I love you" to everyone. Her last words on the tape are "good-bye." It's so beautiful! We'll always treasure it. I just wanted you to know, though, how very, very special that song was to Alison and *is* to us. And YOU are, too!

I wept when I came to the end of the letter. But I thanked God for the privilege He gave me to brighten Alison's life a little—and, in some small measure, to share in her suffering. That was hard, but perhaps by doing it in spite of the difficulty, I would learn to do even more for other little girls like Ali.

Almost two months went by before I answered Sylvia Zach's letter. I didn't want to pass off some conventional condolences and leave it at that. I wanted to share myself honestly and perhaps say something of real strength and consolation to her. Anyway, I finally got my attempt at all this in the mail about a week before Easter. Sylvia's answer came back quickly. It contained such a touching testimony of the way God comforts us that I want to share parts of it as well.

April 13, 1979

Dear Debby,

A very wonderful thing happened today, Good Friday. I received a beautiful letter from a very special lady—you! I was so surprised and thoroughly delighted.

The girls and I had been out doing some last-minute Easter shopping, and when we came home the mail was waiting. What a beautiful thing to read just before going to Good Friday services. I felt so thankful to God for making you the wonderful person you are.

After Ali died, I was deeply despondent and devastated, almost to the point of desperation. I kept praying to God to give me a sign—anything, even just a feeling of inner peace. I even asked Jesus to come into my life in a new way, to take over completely. But the peace I was seeking just did not seem to come.

I told Fr. Richard, the Catholic chaplain from Roswell Park, about it. He felt very badly, but the only advice he could give me was just to keep on praying, which I did.

Then one day . . . I was very down. We received a note from Fr. Richard that day which helped a little, but not really enough. Later, I was doing laundry in the utility room, crying a little, and I found something which has given me the peace I sought. My sign!

I have to digress and explain that almost two years ago, in July, for Ali's fifth birthday, she received a beautiful gold bracelet and gold cross with a diamond in it from her godfather. She begged me to let her wear it. I said, "No, you'll lose it." Well, she begged and pleaded and I gave in with the warning that "if you lose it, you're in trouble!"

Sure enough, a short time later she came in crying. The chain had broken and she had lost the cross. I made all the kids go outside and look for it. Can you imagine trying to find a tiny, gold cross on a hot, sunny July day—in the grass, yet!

Well, they found the broken chain, but no cross. In the nearly two years that followed, I had just about forgotten about it. I'm sure you can guess what it was that I found that day. Alison's cross! My sign from God!

For some reason, my clothes dryer was out of place, and as I bent to fix it my eye caught a bright, shiny object on the floor behind the dryer. I knew immediately what it was, even before I picked it up. And when I did pick it up, I swear, Debby, the little cross almost burned a hole in the palm of my hand. I just shook all over with joy.

The next day, and ever since, I've had a curious sense of peace. I hope I'm not psyching myself into all of this. I think not, because I asked God for a sign—it could have been anything—but why that cross that had been gone for so long? Ali's cross! He put it there for me to find. I've had it blessed and wear it always now. When I feel low, I just hang on to it.

Yes, I do still have some very bad days. But, I know in my heart that Alison is okay, and I just have to keep on believing that I *will* see her again. I couldn't go on living if I did not believe that! It's just that I miss her so much and long to see her.

The letter went on for two more pages after that. I felt honored to be part of God's plan in another person's life. Sylvia's story encouraged me.

As I thanked God for the way He had given Sylvia her sign, a thought came to me. I reached for my purse, pulled out my wallet, and found a photograph. It was of a little girl named Karey. I had not yet met her. I had gotten the picture from her aunt in St. Louis the previous summer. I'll tell the story from the beginning.

"Miss Boone, may I speak with you for a moment?"

I cringed as the woman walked toward me. I was backstage in St. Louis. In a little while, I would be onstage with Daddy. I needed to get ready. Somehow this lady had found her way to me, and I felt trapped.

"Yes, what can I do for you?"

"I have a niece who's very sick in the hospital, going through radiation. Her name is Karey Addison, and she's only seven years old."

"Oh, that's awful. I'm so sorry."

"She just loves you and your song so much. Here's a picture of her that she wanted me to give you. Do you think you could send her an autographed picture of yourself? It would mean so much to her."

"Of course, I can. In fact, I have a few pictures right here. If I sign one for Karey right now, would you send it off to her for me?"

"Oh, thank you. She'll be so pleased. Thank you so much."

After she left, I looked at the child's picture. There was the endearing face of a sweet child. Unlike most children, though, Karey was wearing a blonde wig to cover the loss of hair caused by the radiation treatments. She was obviously very frail. It broke my heart to think of all she must be going through.

I took the picture with me and went to my dad's dressing room for our usual time of prayer before the show.

"Look at this, Daddy. This little girl is very sick—some kind of cancer, I think. Her aunt just gave me the picture. Can we include her in our prayers tonight?"

"Sure." Daddy looked briefly at the photo, laid it aside, and took my hand.

"Dear Father, we pray for this little girl, Karey. We ask You to comfort her and her family in a special way right now. Step into her life and touch her with Your healing power. We ask this in Jesus' name."

I picked up the picture and put it in my purse. Her address was on the back. She was in Orange, California. That was close enough to my home that I could contact her. I made a mental note to give her a call when I got back to southern California.

But when I got home, things were busier than ever, and my good intentions fell by the wayside. Yet, somehow, I couldn't forget Karey. I thought of and prayed for her often, but I felt sort of helpless, not knowing more about her. Did her family know the Lord? Did she believe Jesus could help her? Was she surrounded by faith or unbelief? I didn't know. I was thankful, however, that the Lord had put her on my heart. I prayed that His peace would envelop her entirely and that she would know and feel His presence very strongly.

Then, one Sunday morning not long after I received the news of Alison Zach's death, I met Karey accidentally. I had gone to Robert Schuller's church in Orange County to sing in the morning service. I was standing on the platform—which stands rather high above the congregation—singing a song called "You Took My Heart By Surprise." When I scanned the sea of faces below me, I saw her! That little face was beaming up at me. I recognized her immediately from the picture I still had in my wallet.

As soon as Pastor Schuller gave the benediction, I ran downstairs to meet her. There she was with that sweet little smiling face. Two women had accompanied her to the service. They were, I quickly learned, her mother and a nurse from the hospital.

I knelt on one knee to say hello to little Karey. Before I knew it, she was perched contentedly on my other knee. A sweet quietness enfolded both of us in that moment. I felt so close to her that it was as if I'd always known her.

With hardly a word, she gazed straight into my eyes. Those eyes—I had never seen eyes so peaceful. I knew God had answered my prayer. The thought excited me. I also knew without a doubt that God had sent this little girl into my life, and me into her life, for a special purpose.

After talking a few minutes, we hugged and kissed each other. I hated to leave her.

"Karey, I'm going to do my best to come and see you again real soon. I promise."

I hugged her one last time and said goodbye. I had to travel to the other end of Los Angeles County by early afternoon. On the flight north via helicopter, I told Gabri all about Karey. (He had been with me at Dr. Schuller's church, but not when I went down to see Karey.) We agreed we would both go see her soon.

Just a few weeks later, Gabri and I had a day free to drive down to Orange County and visit Karey in the hospital. Her mother had told her there would be a surprise that day, but not that I was coming. I'll never forget the way her face lit up when we walked into the room.

"Hi, Karey. I told you I'd see you soon."

Karey was sitting up in bed. That day she was not wearing

a wig, and she was hooked up to an I.V. unit. The seriousness of her condition became more real to me than ever, and so did my desire to help in any way I could.

"Oh, boy! Debby! I didn't know you were coming! What's that?"

I was holding a big stuffed animal. It was the fuzziest, softest, most wonderful bear cub ever. It looked almost lifelike.

"This is Laszlo, Karey. He's lived with me for about two years . . . except for about two weeks, when he stayed with my sister, Cherry, in the hospital. I found him in Oslo, Norway, and brought him back to the United States. I felt kind of funny about buying a Teddy bear, but I just had to—he wouldn't let me leave without him. Now I know he wants to be a special friend to you in the hospital."

I put Laszlo down on Karey's little lap, and she nestled happily into his soft fur. "Thanks, Debby. I love Laszlo. He's the nicest bear I ever met. How did he get his name? Did you give it to him?"

"Well, not exactly. I felt a little silly when I brought him home from my trip. I think my dad saw how I felt. Anyway, he was the one who thought of the name."

Karey and I loved being together. She showed me all the pictures she had of the day we met at church, and I told her that Gabri and I had just become engaged. She felt a little special when I told her she was one of the first to know.

The next thing I knew, I was hearing a recording of myself singing. I turned to look. It came from a cassette player in the lap of a little girl who came riding into the room in a little red wagon. Pretty soon, several of Karey's friends from the children's oncology unit were making their way into Karey's room to meet Gabri and me. The news of our visit had traveled fast. Parents and nurses were huddled outside the door, and I found myself in the midst of about a half dozen children. We were all singing "You Light Up My Life," with the children knowing the words as well as I did. At first, it was heartbreaking to see them singing their little hearts out.

Several were bald from chemotherapy. Most of them were underweight and had dark circles under their eyes. But as we all sang together, I saw such love shining from each of their faces that I felt like lifting my hands right then and thanking God for using me and my music to bring joy into the lives of children like these.

Even though Karey was hooked up to intravenous tubes, she managed to move far enough to sit first in my and then in Gabri's lap. It was love at first sight between her and Gabri. She got a first-class, old-fashioned crush on him that day, and it never went away.

Later, Gabri and I walked around the ward to various rooms to visit the children who couldn't get out of bed. As we drove back to Los Angeles that afternoon, I was thinking a lot about what we'd seen. And I thought about Sylvia Zach's second letter that had encouraged me so much. My faith was growing, somehow, through all this. Before we got out of the car, Gabri took my hand and began to pray aloud: "Heavenly Father, Debby and I do want You to heal Karey. Please show us what we're supposed to do and say and how we can really be used by You in this situation. In the name of Jesus, we pray."

"Amen," I agreed.

That day, Gabri and I had entered into a serious commitment to Karey. It was a responsibility neither of us took lightly. There were times when I wondered if I had bitten off more than I could chew. I was pretty inexperienced when it came to exercising my faith in the area of healing, and I still had many questions about faith and how it operated. What if her family got their hopes up and trusted in me and what I said; and then Karey, for some reason or another, didn't make it? I could make things worse, instead of better. But the Lord helped me to realize that He had put a real love for Karey in my heart. He was the Healer, and His Word had a lot of promises for those who believed. I was going to find out what the Lord wanted me to do and commit myself to do it, no matter what.

After reading Scriptures such as, "These signs will accompany those who believe: . . . they will lay their hands on the sick, and they will recover" (Mark 16:17,18) and ". . . I am the LORD your healer" (Exodus 15:26), my position seemed pretty clear. Gabri agreed that we were to believe God for Karey's healing and speak words of faith to Karey and her family. We did just that. On several occasions, when Karey was at home, Gabri and I visited and prayed with Karey, her mother, and her grandmother. We all prayed for perfect health for Karey, believing in the Lord's power to bring this about.

Once, the Lord gave me an idea in prayer that gave us a real focus for our faith. The idea was that I ask Karey to be the flower girl in our wedding. This gave us all something to look forward to and work towards. We could see in our minds a healthy, beautiful little girl walking down the aisle. That picture was important to hold onto at times when Karey was at her worst. Mary, Karey's mother, was thrilled with the idea, but nobody was more excited than Karey. I knew she understood the deeper purpose of the invitation.

Karey met everyone in my family at one time or another. One afternoon she, her mother, her sister, and one of her brothers came to see us taping a family TV special. My family fell in love with her. Karey, obviously being inclined to crushes, got a crush on my father one night when she and her parents spent the night in our home. We found out Karey had the capacity to fall in love with several guys at once. First it was Gabri, and then my dad, but one of the sweetest things I ever heard Karey say was that she wanted Jesus to be her boyfriend.

Eventually Karey's condition worsened and she lapsed into a coma. Thereafter I kept in touch almost daily. Some days her vital signs were up. Other times they were down. I struggled to keep steady in faith and not to respond too strongly to these ups and downs. It was hard, and I prayed often for little Karey.

About a week later, on my way home from a short concert tour, I got word from my mother that Karey had died. At first

I was stunned and confused. Why couldn't she have lived and been there at my wedding—a walking testimony to God's power and grace? How could God be glorified now, with things the way they were?

Suddenly, I felt the presence and comfort of the Lord, who seemed to be saying, "Debby, you've been faithful through all of this. Don't give up your faith now. Look to Me, not to the circumstances."

As I thought and prayed about what had happened and why, the Holy Spirit brought me comfort and proof of God's faithfulness through all of this. I thought of different instances of healing in the Bible where the Lord asked the sick person: "Do you want to be healed?" Of course, Karey had told us that she wanted to be well, but when the Holy Spirit poses the question, He always gets the truth.

Perhaps when Karey was in the coma the Lord asked her that question. I have heard many stories about people who saw the Lord at times like that. Is it possible He came to Karey and gave her a choice? What if she *had* seen Him face to face? I thought about her crushes on Gabri and my dad, and about the time when she told me she wanted Jesus to be her favorite boyfriend. She was seven years old when she died; she had been sick since she was three. The treatments had been almost as bad as the disease. The pain had been incredible at times. What if this seven-year-old child had been faced with a choice between returning to the world she had known and living forevermore with the most beautiful, loving "boyfriend" she had ever met?

Would choosing heaven have been selfish of Karey? I thought of the words of St. Paul. Writing from a prison cell, he had said, "For to me to live is Christ, and to die is *gain*. If it is to be life in the flesh, that means fruitful labor for me. Yet which I shall choose I cannot tell. I am hard pressed between the two. *My* desire is to depart and be with Christ, for that is *far better*" (Philippians 1:21–23, italics mine).

Even a mature believer in the Lord like Paul had a hard time choosing between life here and life in heaven. Karey's death gave me a new appreciation for Paul's words. Always before they had seemed pretty distant to me. I had a hard time thinking of death as something to rejoice in. I now began to see, however, that chronic serious pain and suffering—which had not been a significant part of my life—had a way of making this life seem less attractive. The promise of eternal life through Jesus' resurrection and ascension began to take on more substance for me after Karey's death.

Still, after this experience, could I expose myself to pain and death like this again? At the Lord's leading, definitely yes. Before I recorded "You Light Up My Life," I was involved with troubled children at Hathaway. Then the Lord led me to Alison, Karey, and others like them. I've never been able to explain why, but I have unusual rapport with little children.

I believe God has called me, in part at least, to be with children and to help them. And, I believe, there will be those who are healed and restored to strength here and now—and many who will come to faith in Christ as a consequence. In the meantime, I'm learning about faith. I can't allow my faith to be based on past experiences. Instead my faith is in God, who is the same yesterday, today, and forever. My responsibility is to walk in trusting obedience, to do what I sense the Lord is telling me, to rely on His forever unchanging Word, and to leave the results with Him.

I was learning to make commitments, and that felt good.

The Wedding

Not long after Karey died, I began to devote my full attention to the wedding. Gabri and I and our parents had lots to do. We had already scheduled our busy pastor, Jack Hayford, to perform the ceremony at the Hollywood Presbyterian Church. We decided this church was more accessible to many of our guests and was nearer to the Wilshire Country Club, where the reception would be held, than was our own church building in Van Nuys.

Donna would be my maid of honor. Gabri asked his brother Miguel to be his best man. Young Donavan Freberg would be the ring bearer, and Hannah Cutrona, the eight-year-old daughter of our friends, Henry and Nona Cutrona, would be the flower girl. We decided to keep the wedding party small, and so there were no other bridesmaids.

On Wednesday night, just three days before the Saturday afternoon wedding, Donna Freberg hosted a small bridal shower for me. It was different from any shower I'd been to before. The seven guests—my mother among them—showered me with spiritual gifts instead of material gifts. Each of the guests offered special wisdom and prayers for Gabri and me, for our life together, for any children we might have, for our home and work. My mother told me she believed God intended to establish Gabri and me as examples of His standard for marriage in the midst of a society that is taking marriage and family life less seriously every day.

During the two remaining days before the wedding, I

noticed I was enjoying an underlying cushion of peace in spite of the normal bridely nervousness. I was in good spirits, and things that usually might have angered or upset me seemed unimportant. I thanked God for the special gift of Donna's shower many times in those hectic days.

I awoke Saturday morning with that indescribable combination of awe, joy, and excitement that is, I'm sure, common to most brides. I hadn't been up long, however, before my mood was interrupted.

"Debby?" Daddy's familiar call came down the hall from a room we used as a studio in the house.

"Yes, Daddy, what is it?"

"Would you come here for a moment?"

"What's up?" I asked as I rounded the corner and entered the room.

"I just remembered that we've got to do some radio spots for that Japanese tour coming up next month. And . . . well, you and Gabri will be away on your honeymoon. It'll be too late to do them when you get back. So, I guess we should do them this morning," he said, grinning.

"Right now?" I could hardly believe my ears.

"Why not? You don't have anything else to do today, do you?" he asked, laughing.

Then I began to laugh. The look on Daddy's face, the absurdity of it all, and the fact that I really didn't have much to do for the next hour until it was time to get away to the church—all struck me at once. Actually, Daddy was in a bigger hurry than I. He still had to shower and get dressed after two hours of tennis with Mike Curb that morning! Anyway, we got down to business and recorded the spots.

My lightheartedness persisted throughout the day. Donna got to my house in time to catch a ride with me to the church, as planned. But, as we headed out the driveway. . . .

"Oh, no!" Donna gasped.

"What's the matter?" I asked.

"I can't believe it. I forgot my purse."

"Well, we'll just have to turn around and go by your house to pick it up." I couldn't believe my own calmness.

When we did arrive at the church about a half an hour late, I was glad to have someone there to do my hair for me. Then I did my makeup and even finished Donna's for her. Two o'clock, the hour appointed for our guests to arrive, came and went, and still I wasn't dressed. There must have been a hundred buttons down the back of that gown, and there was no way to speed up the buttoning process. They had to be done one at a time. The ceremony did not begin until 2:45.

Meanwhile, Gabri was enduring his own problems. As far as he was concerned, things were pretty much on schedule. He had no clue that I was running late. Miguel and he had driven to the church in plenty of time. Miguel was even more nervous than Gabri was. Then, as they were getting into their suits. . . .

"Oh great," Miguel sounded dismayed.

"What's the matter?" Gabri asked.

"Look, these pants are too short!"

He was right. They were a good two inches above the tops of his shoes.

"What am I gonna do?" Panic was in his voice now.

"Sue the tailor?"

"C'mon, really."

"Okay, okay. Look, they're not that short. Pull them down as much as you can and button your jacket. No one'll notice."

Gabri assured him the results of this procedure were acceptable. Miguel seemed relieved.

About ten minutes before 2:00, Pastor Jack joined them. He, too, it turned out, was unaware of the lack of progress in the women's dressing area. He gave Gabri and Miguel last-minute instructions, talking as if there was little time to lose. "Okay, it's almost time. Your cue to come out onto the platform from the side door will be when you hear the organ stop playing. There will be an interval of silence, and the string quartet will play the processional music. Got it?"

"Got it."

"Good. It's 2:00 now. Things should get underway in about ten minutes. I'll be coming in from the other side, so I'll see you out there."

"Okay," they said as he strode away.

Miguel and Gabri turned and walked over to the door through which they would walk out onto the platform. They stood there in silence, listening to the organ music for a long time. Suddenly, the organ stopped. Gabri looked at his watch. It was almost 2:25.

Miguel spoke up, "Well, looks like this is it," and he reached out to open the door.

"Wait a second. Let's make sure," Gabri said. Five seconds, then ten went by. The organ remained silent.

"Okay, this is it. Let's go." The next thing they knew, they were looking into a sea of five hundred faces, an awful lot of which were familiar to them. Their arrival created a hush of expectancy, but the quartet did not start playing. And where was Pastor Jack? They stood smiling and nodding to various people who were waving their greetings.

Then the organ music resumed, playing music obviously suited for a prelude. Instantly, Miguel and Gabri realized they had made a mistake. Miguel leaned over, "What should we do?"

"I don't know. Let me think."

The seconds ticked away and pretty soon it was embarrassingly obvious to everyone that they weren't supposed to be there. Gabri looked at his watch, 2:30. He then turned to Miguel and shrugged. Miguel shrugged back and they awkwardly backed away toward the door. They hammed it up a little and got a good laugh before they were back in the waiting area.

Miguel and Gabri joked a few moments about the mix-up, and then Miguel began to shake his head. "I can't do it to you. I just can't do it to you," he said.

"What can't you do to me?" Gabri asked.

"Look at the bottom of your shoes."

He pulled his left foot up to his right knee to see the bottom of his shoe. There, in white tape, was the word "Help." He checked the bottom of the other shoe and found the word "me." Gabri and I would be kneeling for prayer and communion toward the end of the ceremony. The platform was high enough that most of the people in the room would have been able to see that plea for help on the bottoms of his shoes. He thanked Miguel as he peeled the tape off.

A few moments later, the organ stopped again. It was almost 2:45. They peeked out the door and could see the stringed quartet getting ready to play. So, they sauntered back onto the platform, evoking more laughter from the guests.

The quartet waited for a little quiet and struck up the processional music. Soon, I was coming down the aisle toward them on my dad's arm. The walk down the aisle was nerveracking. My bouquet was pretty heavy, and I was trembling. But all of our guests appeared so warm and friendly as I passed by that they melted away much of my tension.

Shortly, Gabri, Daddy, and I were standing before Pastor Jack. Daddy was on my left, Gabri on my right. Jack smiled and looked down at the assembled guests.

"It is not only my privilege to welcome you on behalf of the bride and the groom and their families, but to announce to you that it is precisely 2:00, Boone standard time." Laughter. He continued, "Gabri is still seeking to help Debby adjust to where the rest of us live." More laughter. "Most of you saw him arrive and then find out he still had time to go out and grab a Big Mac, some fries, and a large Coke. Really, though, you find about half of your work done for you, as one officiating at a ceremony, when you have something happen as did a moment ago when Gabri and Miguel came out. It somehow has a way of releasing us from an undue sense of obligation to the ceremonial. I don't mean by that that we take these moments lightly, but they are intended to be very fulfilling and happy moments—not just in a sentimental way, but in a thoroughly biblical way."

Jack went on to recall how Jesus had blessed marriage by attending the wedding at Cana. Jack explained that whenever Jesus is invited into ordinary human situations, the extraordinary happens. He then asked everyone to join hands to indicate their agreement while he prayed, inviting Jesus to attend our wedding and to make something extraordinary of it.

After the prayer, when everyone was seated, Jack continued. "The same thing that I ask for myself when our children marry, my friend Pat has asked: the privilege of not only giving, in this case, the hand of a daughter to the groom, the man who's to be the man of her life, but of speaking a prayer of paternal benediction over this new home. . . . God has not ceased the patriarchal system. He intends for fathers to minister the life and authority of the kingdom. And now, in the transfer of that leadership to another man, he passes his daughter on, not only with a word, but with a prayer. Shall we join in prayer as Pat leads us."

Daddy prayed, "Lord God, we love You today. Our hearts are full, overflowing. We know, Lord, You're the source of our happiness, the source of our fulfillment, the source of our lives themselves. And we thank You, and we praise You from the depths of our beings. You've been so good to us. I thank You for this girl—her life, her glow, her voice, her spirit. I thank You, Lord, that You've shared her with us for these years and brought her to blossom and to bloom in our midst. I thank You, Lord, for this young man, Gabriel—my friend and my brother. It's no accident that these two lives have been woven together. You've done that. We relax in it and we glorify You in it, and we look for great things from this union today.

"Lord, under Your authority, because You've made me father of this bride, because I belong to You, I do speak a blessing. A blessing of long life, of fruitfulness, of impact for good on millions, of deep inner happiness, of true oneness, of healthy children, of fun, of joy, of music—human and spiritual music—throughout their lives together. And I commend them now into Your care and to each other for eternity. In Jesus' name, amen."

After that, Pastor Jack brought Gabri and me up onto the platform to exchange our vows. But first, my soon-to-be mother-in-law beautifully sang "The Promise." Its refrain

spoke words of commitment which less than a year before I
had felt unable to make. But now, I praised God, they were a
true expression of my whole being.

> *Say goodbye?*
> *Why, I can barely say goodnight.*
> *If I can hardly take my eyes from yours,*
> *How far could I go?*
>
> *Walk away?*
> *The thought would never cross my mind.*
> *I couldn't turn my back on spring or fall*
> *Your smile least of all.*
>
> *When I say always, I mean forever.*
> *I trust tomorrow as much as today.*
> *I am not afraid to say I love you—*
> *And I promise you I'll never say goodbye.*
>
> *We're dancers on a crowded floor*
> *While other dancers live from song to song*
> *Our music goes on—on and on.*
>
> *And if I never leave your arms*
> *I really will have travelled everywhere*
> *For my world is there.*
>
> *When I say always, I mean forever.*
> *I trust tomorrow as much as today.*
> *I am not afraid to say I love you—*
> *And I promise you I'll never say goodbye.*
> *How could I ever say goodbye?**

And so, as Gabri and I stood face to face, holding both
hands, we spoke lifelong vows with joy and gladness.

. . .So Far

The year that followed our wedding was an unusually full and eventful time. Three months after we got back from our honeymoon, I taped my first TV special. It aired in the spring of 1980 to generally positive reviews and a top-twenty Nielsen rating.

Also during this three-month period I became an expectant mother. The demands of pregnancy slowed me down sufficiently to devote serious attention to the writing of this book. It has been hard. I have often felt as if I were back in high school with an enormous term paper assignment hanging over my head.

When I first learned I was pregnant—not so very long after our wedding—I was surprised. And a little upset. It wasn't part of the plan. Gabri and I had talked about it, and we agreed it would be a good idea to wait two or three years before we started raising a family. After all, we were still very young, and with my busy schedule we had wanted to save any spare time for just the two of us.

Right? Wrong!

One of the biblical proverbs says, "Many are the plans in the mind of a man, but it is the purpose of the LORD that will be established" (Proverbs 19:21). God had been overruling my plans now and again for as long as I could remember! It finally dawned on me how foolish I was to think He might stop now that I was married.

Besides, I could look back on every previous occasion in which I had been overruled and see that the way in which God had led me instead inevitably led to good things. So, I rejected the temptation to feel a little sorry for myself, and, gradually, found I was genuinely happy—even excited—about being pregnant.

Our little boy, Jordan Alexander, was born on July 8, 1980, strong and healthy. On July 27, we took him to church to be dedicated to the Lord. Our pastor, Jack Hayford, took Jordan from our arms and playfully held him up for all to see. Then he invited Gabri to pray.

"Father," Gabri began, "we thank You that, as Solomon wrote long ago, children are the heritage of the Lord, and the fruit of the womb is His reward. But we are very aware this morning, that without Your help we cannot be the parents You want us to be.

"You have commanded, Father, that every male which opens the womb shall be called holy to the Lord. So, as Hannah dedicated Samuel, as Mary dedicated Jesus, we dedicate our firstborn to You. We declare to this congregation, to the heavenly hosts, and to the satanic powers, that Jordan is the Lord's property.

"We pronounce the blessings of the firstborn on him, even asking for a double portion for him. And, Lord Jesus, we appeal to You as the firstborn among many brethren, to watch over Jordan and to keep him from every evil."

Gabri went on to ask that Jordan would increase in wisdom and stature, and in favor with God and men. Then he asked wisdom for us, the parents, to raise him properly. He particularly asked grace for himself not to provoke Jordan to anger or discouragement, but to be diligent to discipline him and drive out the foolishness which the Bible says is naturally "bound up" in the heart of a child. He concluded by thanking God for the congregation that was, in this very ceremony, dedicating itself to help us raise Jordan. And, last of all, he thanked Him for Jordan.

Pastor Jack added, "Father God, we agree as a congregation with the commitment these parents have made on behalf of their child. And, in Jesus' name, at their hand, I present to You Jordan Alexander Ferrer. Amen."

Instead of interrupting my relationship with Gabri, the arrival of Jordan has only drawn us more closely together. That has happened in several ways. For one, being parents has given us a way to channel the energy that comes from our relationship toward a common goal. Even more importantly, the experience has drawn both of us closer to God because we have a new recognition of our need for Him to help us pass through new territory.

With my interest in the meanings of names, one would naturally think Gabri and I had researched carefully the meaning of Jordan Alexander's name and chosen it for very specific reasons. In a way we did, but in a way we didn't.

At the beginning of 1980, we met with Pastor Hayford to pray and counsel together about what might lie ahead in the New Year. He told us he sensed the idea of flowing—that God wanted to flow freely in our lives and marriage. And he mentioned that the name of the River Jordan means "to flow." That stuck with me, and when Gabri and I began to discuss names, we found ourselves favoring Jordan strongly. Alexander means "defender of men." I like that. We are waiting to see what the names will mean precisely in the case of our firstborn.

I stayed home with Jordan for the first three months after he was born, but then, gradually, it was back to work. Not that those three months were pure vacation. In addition to tending to our new baby, Gabri and I continued working regularly on the completion of this book. But, in October 1980 it was back to the work of entertaining. As far as I can objectively assess both marriage and career—and the way in which those two things are bound closely together—we have both pretty successfully moved into our nontraditional roles.

Gabri likes to cook and he does it well. I do better at cleaning up the kitchen. Neither of us is crazy about changing diapers, but, as Eleanor Roosevelt once said, "One finds that what one must do, one usually can do." And, with the help of a once-a-week housekeeper, we both manage to keep the house semi-decent and in order.

Gabri is a gentle and practical man. He has unusual perceptiveness in the midst of most all situations. He is very single-minded, not easily thrown off course. Yet he doesn't ramrod his way through. He just quietly persists with what he perceives to be the truth. His steady disposition has helped me through a treacherous passage. The unprecedented popularity of "You Light Up My Life" was, I knew from the first, impossible to duplicate. Yet, for quite a while, I felt pressure from within and without to try, somehow, to top it. Eventually I recognized the truth that the path away from 1978 would be less spectacular—for a while at least.

Sometimes singers enjoy a meteoric rise in their careers. They may have five big hits in a row. But after that, it's possible they'll drop out of sight for good.

There are other entertainers who are there year after year after year. They produce and keep producing a quality product. Their careers may be marked by occasional spectacular successes, but those successes are not the substance of their careers. Lying beneath is a solid, steady flow of good music—winter, spring, summer, and fall, year in and year out. These are the entertainers who become known to the public as a person, rather than a name. That's what I want. They have a relationship with the people they entertain and they enjoy the loyalty of real fans—people who stick with them over the years because they're genuinely interested.

With Gabri's help, I'm beginning to outlive my meteoric beginning and to settle into something more lasting and substantial. A lot of nice things have happened along the way. A big event was getting invited by Frank Sinatra to be part of the cast of entertainers who helped President-elect Reagan celebrate his inaugural eve gala. In March and April 1981, I was especially honored to receive a Grammy and then a Dove award for my first solo gospel album, *With My Song.*

Dove awards are bestowed by the Gospel Music Association in Nashville. Receiving one represents part of the direction my career has been taking, namely into the realm of music with explicitly Christian content. In *With My Song* I attempted to express serious worship and to encourage worship in the hearts of the listeners. We looked long and hard for songs that would serve this purpose. It took nearly a year before I was ready to record the album.

Another avenue along which my career has traveled is that of country music. After "You Light Up My Life" had run its course on the pop charts in 1978, it began to appear on the country charts and, so, enjoyed a kind of second wind. This reminded me to look back at my roots in the hills of Tennessee. I am, after all, Red Foley's granddaughter. I have since recorded a number of country albums, and I've been grateful for the warm reception they've received.

As Gabri and I look into the future, then, we're endeavoring to make wise decisions that will make me a stronger and more versatile entertainer. At this point it looks as though that may even take me into drama and other stage work, which will require more of me than singing only. But talk about the future is always speculative. And it all serves to reinforce the lesson I keep re-learning—not to lean on my own understanding but to trust in the Lord.

Meanwhile, I'm still on the road much of the time, though not as much as I would be if I were not a mother. Most of the time, Jordan accompanies us on trips. Other times his two grandmothers share the duty, along with a wonderful nurse God has provided. I trust that, by the time Jordan is ready to start school, I will not be traveling nearly as much as I am now.

In an attempt to bring our lives as up to the minute as I can in light of the publication date of this book, I'm struck again by the impossibility of bringing my story to any sort of resounding conclusion.

Instead, this is the story of Debby Boone Ferrer . . . *so far*. It is the story of a strong-willed child with more than her share of foolishness bound up in her heart, who was determined to make her mark by her own might and main. But she ran into obstacle after obstacle that repeatedly showed her the folly of her own way. And slowly, the grace of God helped her to find that path of humility, submission, and obedience in His way—the wise way.

As I began this story struggling against my father's—and all other—authority, I now end it, having learned to kneel before the head of all authority, my heavenly Father.